CW00666116

ANDY McCOY

SHERIFF McCOY

SHERIFF McCOY

ANDY McCOY

OUTLAW LEGEND OF HANOI ROCKS

TRANSLATED BY
IKE VIL

Bazillion Points

DEDICATED TO

My beloved and hardworking wife,
ANGELA MCCOY–NICOLETTI
Thanks for everything you've put up with.

USTED KAMAN
an Afghan music legend who
dedicated his life to fighting
fascism, racism, terrorism, and,
in the end, the Taliban,
with music.

JUDY

KATALLE

© Andy McCoy and WSOY, 2001
All rights reserved.
Original title <u>Sheriffi McCoy</u>
First published by WSOY in 2001,
Helsinki, Finland
Graphic design by J. S. Karjalainen

Supervised for Bazillion Points by Ian Christe
Edited by Polly Watson
English translation by Ike Vil
Published in the United States in 2009
Bazillion Points Publishing, Brooklyn, NY
ISBN 978 0 9796163 0 3
Printed in China

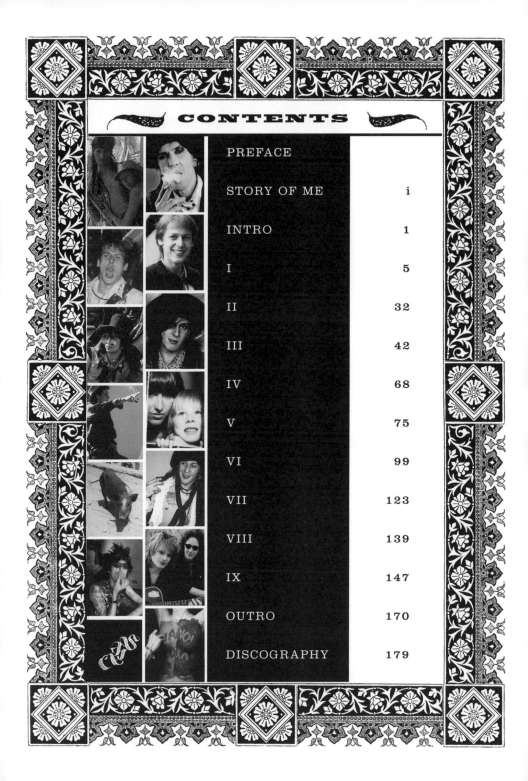

CONTENTS

PREFACE

Tokyo, 2009

What you are about to read is a small summary of things and happenings in my distant past. I recently reread this book, and one thing I'm sure of is that it would not be written the way it is if I had written it now. Certain priorities and values in life are way more important to me nowadays than they were back then. I don't wanna cash in on other people's misery, but at that time I think so many people were cashing into mine that I wanted payback.

If sleaze is what you want—and none of it exaggerated—then you get that with this book. Only in this case, the stories are as true as when they were documented. As are all the beautiful things stated. Most of them are a matter of public record.

Today's youth tend to glamorize the ugly things in life. I am way beyond that, soon to be hitting fifty. I am just fed up with the baby shit. People think they are living in a video game. They seem to think they can shoot someone for real, and afterwards the victim will still come up and congratulate them on a good shot. Something that is so far from my life, at least.

This book is only entertainment for entertainment's sake, for lovers of rock 'n' roll history and people who have a taste for the macabre. Anyway, I hope you have a good read, and remember: this is my truth, you have your truth, and there is the universal truth. I try to balance between all of them.

VILLE JUURIKKALA

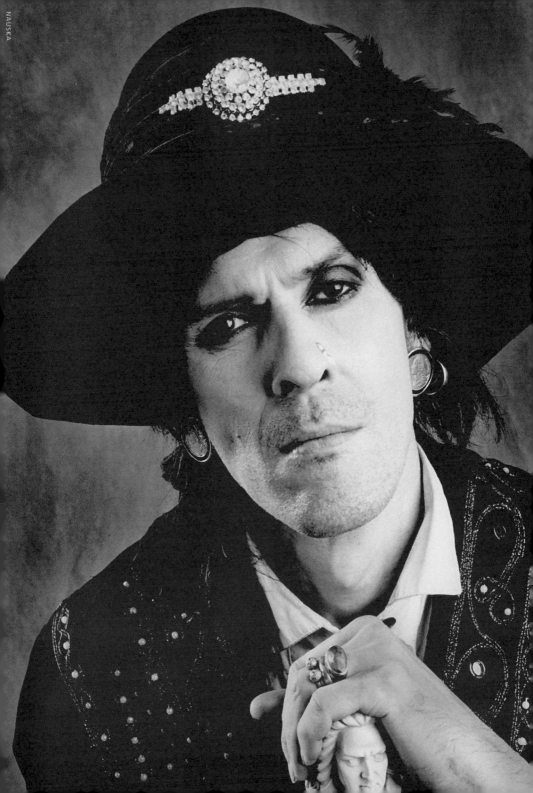

NAUSKA

STORY OF ME

Obligatory class essay, Östra Svenska Läroverket:

Hi, my name is Antti Hulkko. I was born fifteen autumns ago (October 11, 1962) in the village of Pelkosenniemi, on the banks of the Kemi River in Northern Finland. My mother tongues are Finnish and Swedish. I've mastered both languages, but I'm more fluent in Swedish. My school is Botby Högstadieskola (used to be Östra Svenska Läroverket) and I'm in the ninth class, the last before high school. The school is located in Puotinharju, Helsinki, four miles or fifteen minutes by bus from my home in Vuosaari. In addition to what I've been taught in school, I also learned practical English when we were living in Stockholm, Sweden, where my best friend's family spoke English. We moved to Stockholm from Oulu in 1964 and lived there until last autumn (1976) when we came back to Finland.

I'm interested in parapsychology and Oriental culture (mysticism). But I guess I wouldn't call them my hobbies, firstly because it's not that often that I dabble with the aforementioned things, and secondly because I think a hobby should be something for which you sacrifice your whole heart and soul. I'd say my real hobbies are playing guitar and drawing/painting,

because I do those things almost every day. I've
played guitar since I was five, everything from Mozart
to Abba. I play in a band, and we're currently making
punk rock records. My biggest gig so far was at the
Linnanmäki amusement park this autumn, where our band
performed to fourteen thousand people. It was really
great to be onstage that day (the same stage, by the
way, where Paul Anka once played, the first so-called
big star to visit Finland). Drawing is something I've
done almost all my life. My specialty is shaded pencil
drawings. In Stockholm, my art was even featured in
some exhibitions, but they were so small that they're
not worth mentioning.

I think I'm a happy person by nature. I try to
see the positive and not the negative in things. I
talk...pretty much—too much, according to my friends,
who always try to shut me up. But at the end of the
day, I think I'm still a silent (contemplative) guy.

I have two idols. The first one is Jimi Hendrix,
the best and most impressive electric guitar player
there ever was or will be. His lyrics are also
divine, as they portray today's world in a really
wonderful way. Buy Jimi Hendrix's GREATEST HITS and
see for yourself. My other idol is Marc Bolan, who
just died a few weeks ago, by the way. His voice is
smooth as velvet and he has something that only great
personalities have—that special something I really
like!

My friends are normal Finnish-Swedish kids.
Almost all of them live in Kulosaari, one of the
neighborhoods of Helsinki. My inner circle of friends
consists of people who play an instrument, draw,
dance, act, or are generally active in the art world
(I feel at home among like-minded people).

I have two siblings. My brother Ilkka is
seventeen and goes to high school at Helsingin I
Normaalikoulu. My sister Eva-Kajsa is twelve, and

she's in the same school with me. My brother also
plays an instrument, bass guitar, and Eva is learning
the piano. My mother, Kaarina, is thirty-six and
works at the Helsinki University Central Hospital.
My father, Risto, is thirty-nine and does some
kind of paper work. He's currently employed as an
organizational consultant.

When I was younger and lived in Stockholm,
I used to play soccer in the little league. I like
sunshine and beaches. In the summer, I take my guitar
and some of Marc Bolan's early albums to the beach.
People often ask me if I'm religious, I mean, do I
believe in Jesus. I usually answer "no," but sometimes
I have the feeling that there must be some kind of
higher power that rules over everything. Personally,
I believe in reincarnation, because it's impossible
that a man's soul would die along with his body. What
do you think yourself? Right now I'm listening to
Marc Bolan's "Fist Heart Mighty Dawn Dart," which is
a pretty good song, by the way. Guitar, vocals, and
bongo drums. But let's move on. I really can't think
of anything else to say about myself, except: I'm 5
foot 6 and I weigh 108 pounds and I'm still growing. I
have dark brown eyes and right now my hair is longish
and between light brown and dark brown.

PSST—I have a couple of curls in my hair.
(And I love living in the city.)

    A N T T I

INTRO

Goa, 1998

I'm sitting here on the balcony of this hotel where we're staying, me and Angela, and trying to figure out a way to begin this book. Here we are, anyway, in Goa, India, watching the waves softly wash on the beach, and I wonder if a guy who's just thirty-six years old—or whatever I'm gonna be when the book's finished—is really old enough to write his own biography. I'm thinking about Hemingway, Burroughs, and the rest. Hell, how could I even think of competing with those guys?

It's true that I've lived a very colorful life, and I'm gonna try my best to give you an idea how it has been. I've had some real good times and also some hard times. I hope that this book will finally clear up some things, so people will realize not everything they read is true. Some stuff has been twisted so much it's insane. Sure, I was a wild boy, but if I had been nearly as wild as legend has it, I'd have died at least a hundred and ten times. Of course I've been in the hospital a couple times, but not for the reasons you might have heard. Hey, in that case I'd be some kind of a medical miracle! So don't believe everything you hear.

1

— MᴄCᴏʏ —

This book was written here and there, all over the world, and I should also say that it was not written in any kind of chronological order. The first chapter might have been written last and so on. These are the things that have come to my mind at a given moment on a given day, and if I came up with something, I would just put it to paper while it was still fresh in my head. I wanted you to have the real facts, not the dope stories I've read about myself and my friends in all these books and magazines. Sometimes they're blown out of all proportion. Sometimes they're downright lies.

I'm basically a pretty normal guy, after all, although I have this special ability. Of course I believe in God, who has granted me a gift that most people can only dream about. I can write music, I can paint, I can be loyal, and that's extremely unusual in the modern entertainment industry. Believe me.

I believe that some guys just get lucky in this business. There's so much criminality involved, I guess I was pretty lucky about that. I started so early, yet nobody really screwed me over big-time, except for a couple of things that I'd rather not talk about. I don't want those people's names mentioned here, but hey—you know who you are. They have concealed their frauds well, and some of that shit has already expired.

The best revenge is to lead a good life, as good as the horrible music business crooks are enjoying. It's a sweeter vengeance to not return their hellos than to beat 'em up, although you sometimes have the urge to do that, too.

They say that everybody and everything's over there in California, right? But that's "Heil Hollywood" propaganda. It's

a city that I sort of hate. Like a sweaty armpit full of heroin and cocaine that's called a city. I sometimes wish that the Big One would finally come, because that place is the twentieth-century Babylon. The home of the greedy. Just when I thought that I'd settle for some "live fast, die young" type of thing, I realized it's total bullshit. I've noticed that when people are happy, they spread good vibes around them.

Somehow I still wound up living in Los Angeles, where the only thing that matters is who you know. Bullshit! Moving back to Europe was the best thing I've ever done. But hey, there are some good sides to L.A., too. I have good friends in La La Land. I just wish they would move away from that old Indian burial ground and quit doing that nasty, impure Mexican heroin that's cheaper than rotgut. Obviously the best thing about L.A.

3

is the fact that I met my wife, Angela, there.

First and foremost, I'd like to thank my wife, Angela McCoy-Nicoletti. Without her, this book would've been impossible to write. Thanks to Aleksi Siltala, Simo Mäenpää, and Kaisa Uusipaikka at WSOY; Sini Perho at Love Kustannus, and Seppo Vesterinen, the first manager of Hanoi Rocks, whom I met through Mike Monroe when I was sixteen or seventeen. Of course I want to thank Michael Monroe, and my brothers Ikke and Danny. In a way, Atte Blom, too, but somehow he's so distant these days. I really don't know what's his problem.

Also thanks to Dave Lindholm and Remu Aaltonen for their friendship. Thanks to my sis, mum, Teukka, the Nicoletti family, Jari and Pentti Fagerholm, Jan Stenfors (*Putosiko kitara?*), and all my friends around the world!

I'd like to dedicate this book to the late Johnny Thunders, who was one of my best friends and also Angela's cousin. It's also dedicated to all the '60s girl groups. And to the memory of Razzle. And to Gene Vincent. And to the memory of Roy Hamilton and Joey Ramone. And to Marc Bolan. And to countless others who gave my life meaning by making music. Maybe one day I can inspire somebody somewhere do what I do now. I mean sharing. That's how I managed to achieve what I want so early in my life. I've tried to live my life to the fullest, but you shouldn't confuse that with burning yourself out, not that "live fast, die young" shit. In any case, I believe this is going to be an interesting trip.

So here we are, and from here we continue to my childhood. Giddyup.

I

I was born in Lapland, Finland, Scandinavia, where the so-called Sami people used to live in ancient times and still do. To my knowledge, the Sami share the same blood with the American Indians. I was born on October 11, in the Year of Our Lord 1962, in the village of Pelkosenniemi, in the shadow of the Year of

A big baby boy—
wow, what a fatso!
A self-portrait.

the Tiger, and the first snow fell on the night I was born. Such beautiful country over there: purity, mountains, forests, all kinds of shit I admire but don't really know, having grown up in the inner city.

The old legends say that when the first snow falls and a baby is born, he will have good luck. That was not the only thing that was weird about the way I came into this world. I appeared from my mother's vulva with my right hand clenched into a fist. Even my grandmother, who was the midwife, wondered whether that little guy thought he was Superman—or *Teräsmies*, as he's called in Finland.

We didn't stick around Lapland for long. It was only supposed to be a vacation before my birth anyway, but I arrived a couple weeks before my time. We first moved to Oulu and later lived all around Northern Europe and Scandinavia.

I was introduced to music by my grandfather. He was a mean musician. He played the mandolin at weddings far and wide, and had mastered the accordion and its Finnish variant, *harmonikka*. Goddamn, he was fast. I couldn't even watch his fingers because they just fuckin' flew over the keys 'til it was all just a blur. The music was really beautiful and just fuckin' kicked ass. I was really impressed.

My grandfather also had these miniature instruments, like a tiny guitar that was perfect for a child's hands. I was allowed to play it when I was about four. Grandpa patiently taught me some chords, and I started picking up all kinds of small stuff.

A lot of kids receive nicknames at school, and me they started calling "Andy." I don't know why, probably because my best friend at the time—he's

GRANDMA AND OPIUM • The 1900s were a crazy time, if you think about my grandmother. Her family came from somewhere in Karelia. Anyway, she marched straight to the pharmacy counter one day and asked for ten grams of opium. They asked what she needed it for, and she said she was in great pain. The pharmacy people were totally blown away that this little old lady would ask for opium, but my grandma was like, "What's the problem?" Man, she hadn't been into a pharmacy since 1910 or something. They told her that opium was a controlled substance, but my grandma insisted that she had been to a pharmacy when she was seventeen, and they had sold her opium right off the bat. The staff went to great lengths to explain her that, you know, times have changed. I guess she sort of lived in the past. She also witnessed with her own eyes the time when Gypsies traveled the country with horse-drawn carts, and how people started settling down. A lot of people still used to live in these small villages, not in the cities like now. I'm a typical child of the inner city and I can be really obnoxious if I want to, but I still know all the social—what do you call them?—skills.

now dead, R.I.P.—was this Jamaican guy called Roy Hamilton. He was a year older than me. I hung out with Jamaican people for the better part of my youth, and I think it was easier for them to say "Andy" than "Antti."

My mother was and still is an angel, but my dad—well, that's a different story. I was the middle child. My little sister, Eva, who's called Kaisa, never did anything wrong. My big brother, Ikke, sometimes did something wrong, but in my father's eyes, everything I did was wrong, and I mean everything. I always got the blame, no matter what happened. He beat me up all the time, and I was blamed for a lot of stuff I didn't do. My father was an alcoholic and an addict, and he cheated on my mother regularly. My mom waited until us kids were old enough; then she left him.

The only nice thing I remember about my father was that he once took me to the swimming hall. It was only this one time, but I felt so proud. And he taught me how to use a knife. Maybe that's why I'm so good at these two things. When my older brother got bigger, we used to beat up the old man together if he started messin' around.

I remember once when I was practicing guitar with my headphones on, and I supposedly made too much noise. My dad struck me so hard on the back of my head that I went out cold. I couldn't hear him coming because I had my headphones on. So he was not a very good man, but *mu huupa san mu huupa*, as they say. My family is my family. It's said that there's not an ethnic group where the majority would be bad, but my father was truly a bad man. If the current welfare authorities even heard rumors of the kind of shit that went down in my family, they'd instantly do something.

In other respects I was pretty much like the rest of the four- or five-year-olds. I had the urge to play soccer every once in a while, but of course I always returned to my guitar.

As I said, I grew up in Stockholm. When I was about seven or eight, I was considered for professional soccer training. AIK Fotboll, one of the biggest soccer teams in Stockholm, had their eye on me, but once again the guitar got the best of me, and slowly soccer faded away from my life. Music and art—painting and drawing—were to be my destiny, it seemed. And it all made me practice like fuck. I think it had an effect on the rest of

The kid's drawing with his sister. About seven or eight years old.

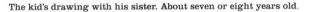

my life, because at that age, seven hours of practice a day can make you good. I set a clock beside me and I played, played, and played. Then I found a really good teacher and got into ragtime and country picking blues. I also learned some advanced classical guitar. I took lessons for a year, but after that he smiled: "Sorry, Andy, I don't know how to say this, but you're already better than me. You should find a new teacher or begin teaching me."

I passed seven years' worth of guitar classes in a single year, and decided that wouldn't be the end of it. I would pursue it further. I had to pursue it, because at the time, I knew nothing about anything else. I still don't.

As a kid, it felt like summers would never end. I used to prance around practically naked and roll on the velvet grass. Sometimes we would drive to Kemijärvi, Pelkosenniemi, where the whole family gathered for summer vacation. I remember when I saw the wilderness of Pyhätunturi for the first time. I was about five, and we climbed all the way up the fell. At that age, it was a pretty awesome and tiring achievement. We saw a mother bear washing her three-month-old cub on the nearby mountain, Noidantunturi. With binoculars it looked as if they were right next to us.

My uncle was still studying at the time, and he used to keep a fire watch on top of Pyhätunturi in northeastern Lapland. I've had no ties to that place since my early childhood, so please don't ask me how it is nowadays. I really don't know.

SOCCER WAS A BIG THING IN STOCKHOLM. There was a lot of fighting over which was the most kick-ass team, and somehow I found myself with the Jamaican guys. Reggae was a big part of their lives, but at that time we didn't even know what pot was.

I hadn't even turned eight when Toufikh, our Moroccan friend, went on holiday in his native Morocco. He was ten years old, and he smuggled back a lump of hash in his mouth. We smoked it and liked it, and afterwards we used to score a little hash for the weekends. We'd play soccer, fight, and jam on the guitar, me and Roy, who had become my best friend, probably the closest friend I've ever had. Unfortunately, he left this world when he was twenty-one. Roy became diabetic later on, and one morning he just forgot to take his injection. He had drawn a bath, and then he had a fit in the tub. Roy's girlfriend sat there for something like twelve hours before she was able to call the cops. She was so devastated that she just cried. She was in total shock. When the ambulance came, Roy was already all blue and bloated. If that girl had immediately called an ambulance or had known the ABC's of first aid, Roy would probably still be alive. Later on I met a guy called Mike who became my best friend post-Roy.

I first became aware of the blues through my own tribe. Roy from Kingston gave me reggae as his legacy, and that's the music I still play at home. Without Roy, I'd never have discovered Bob Marley. Roy's father had been a singer in the '60s and co-owned a studio. When Bob Marley played Stockholm around 1976, he popped into the studio for a visit, and I got to meet the god. *Exodus* had just come out. It was a long, hot summer,

Young Andy and an axe in Stockholm. Notice the
ice hockey game under my ass.

and we used to listen to that album and smoke pot. I had so
many questions I wanted to ask Bob, but I was too freaked out.
Bob just had this massive aura. I had a million things I would've
wanted to ask, but because I was such a huge fan, I turned into
jelly. The only thing that came out of my mouth was: "Pleased
to meet you, sir." He was given one joint after another, and I just
watched from the side. Man, I thought, one day I want to be like
him. A man of wisdom. There's an universal law: Harm no one,
and no one will harm you. That's really idealistic.

I also met Chuck Berry in Stockholm, again completely
by accident. I was something like twelve. I had seen him onstage
a year earlier, probably in the outdoor museum Skansen, or at

maybe Gröna Lund amusement park. I think it was a weekend. I was just walking around the city on a summer day, and there he stood, Mr. Berry. I naturally recognized him and went to ask:

"So, are you Mr. Chuck Berry?"

"Yes, I am," he said.

That was the first time I ever asked for an autograph. I was really impressed. This was in the '70s, and we all wore those freaky, multicolored Afro-American shirts. Hey, after that day, I played my Chuck Berry records even louder than before.

MY DAD BEAT MY MOM, my mom beat my big brother, my big brother beat me, I beat my sister, my sister beat the dog, the dog beat the cat, the cat beat the hamster, and the hamster beat whatever bugs he could find. That was our family's version of the natural order.

I wasn't much into schoolwork. I guess you couldn't call me an A student. There was some good shit and some stupid shit in school, and art and music took over when I was doing my final required year.

Maybe even before that, they knew I wasn't interested in doing the whole year again. The only subjects I was any good in were Swedish, English, music, and art. During science classes and whatnot I just painted in the art room, or played in the music room if it was empty. The teachers sort of accepted the situation, because at least they knew where I was.

I got into some trouble for sure. I think I was four years

old when my father had bought a Mercedes-Benz, the latest model, and parked it outside our house in Stockholm. He had left the keys in the ignition, and I snuck in. Before long I managed to crash the car sideways into a ditch. I ran away, thinking I could never go back home again, but later I got hungry and had to return. I talked to my mom first, and then my dad beat me up, as always. He was drinking and popping pills. Well, yeah, childhood is bliss.

From about ages two through seven, we spent the summers on Bedviksbadet over in Lidingö. That's an island in northern Stockholm that could be reached by an old-fashioned tram at the time. That was really cool. Somebody always had a guitar, and we strummed shit like "Oh la la la Bamba." Some Chuck Berry tunes, too. I always played rhythm and Roy took care of the leads. I was really into playing rhythm—I was proud to do that—but somehow I ended up being a lead guitarist. God knows why. That guy works in mysterious ways, you know. That reminds of something that Isokynä Lindholm once said when a train passed us: "Ding-dong!"

Well, I got into my first band in Stockholm, but we never played live, although we sometimes had something going on in these so-called *ungdomsgården*, these youth centers. Then I learned to my horror that Mom and Dad were planning on moving to Helsinki, Finland. *Stadi*, as they say. Just think about it! Well, I did, and I was like, okay, I guess it's cool by me, if there's a *tunnelbana* in Helsinki, a subway train, a metro. I wanted a real transportation network, because when I was a kid, in the second or third grade, we used to play hooky with a couple of friends and travel around the city on the T-bana. We got to know all these places around Stockholm and hung around a lot at the Kulturhuset, for example.

One remarkable incident was when I saw J. B. Hutto & the Hawks. J. B. Hutto was a black guitarist from Chicago, and I was really curious about the weird metal pipe he used. I went to talk to him, and he told me all about the history of slide guitar and showed me how to tune to E and D. Obviously I've since had to think about the tunings a whole lot more.

So, we moved to Finland, and I realized there was no subway, but it was beautiful late summer. Helsinki was a total enigma for me. I could deal with not having the subway, but a bigger problem was the fact that I spoke almost no Finnish. Well, at least I knew I would be in a Swedish school: *Högsta Svenska Läroverket är det*. The elementary school was located in Botby, and the junior high and high school in Brandö—Kulosaari in Finnish. But when I went to school, I realized I didn't understand their Finnish-Swedish accent at all. Their gibberish sounded like something between Swedish and Finnish. It was pretty weird.

During the first weeks English, art, and music were the only classes where I could understand anything. Otherwise I just sat there, and what little enthusiasm I had for school totally disappeared. I was even supposed to learn a new system of algebra, because we had already learned a more recent system in Stockholm, or whatever—I just remember that at first I learned one system, and then it was changed in the second or third grade. Oh, I don't know. Anyway, bye-bye, mathematics. It also meant forgetting physics and chemistry, and after a while, I just spent my days in the music or art room, although they were other people's classes. But I always went to check out English and history classes.

Each day except Friday I had to take three hours of remedial instruction in Finnish by this older lady called Helga, who also happened to be the headmistress of the school. It was torture. I had to stay with her for three hours after the other kids had gone home, and I was so pissed off. I really envied them. On Fridays I could leave at the same time with the others, so that was okay.

I began to learn Finnish and stuff, but I still had no one to play music with. While I had been living with my parents and my sister in various places, my brother had been raised by our relatives in Finland, and after moving to Helsinki, I actually lived with my brother for the first time. He played the bass and naturally spoke perfect Finnish, so it didn't take long till he had found some friends in Helsinki.

I'll always remember one day looking out the window and seeing my brother talking to this guy who had a big black dog. It was a briard, a French sheepdog. The guy was called Pete, also known as Räkä-Malmi, or Pete Malmi, and he and my brother decided to form a band.

Ikke came home and told me he was in a band, they even had a drummer already, blah blah blah, and I listened with increasing jealousy. Then one day Ikke said that he had told the others what a fuckin' great guitarist I was, although he had never said anything like that to me. Ikke sat there and Pete told me to show them what I got. I played a little of this and that, and Pete said: "Yeah! Fuckin' A! Incredible, where the fuck have you been? You're perfect!" So we got the band going and decided to call it Briard after the black dog that was my first recollection of Pete Malmi. We got a rehearsal place in Töölö.

Sometimes I went to school, sometimes I skipped

Briard live somewhere in Helsinki '77. My notorious, foul-mouthed friend Räkä-Malmi in the front, me in the back, my brother on the bass.

school, and pretty often I hung out with a guy I knew from school called Nasse—later we called him Nasty Suicide. Our home became the headquarters for everybody who was playing hooky, and we'd just spend our days drinking beer and shooting the shit. Meanwhile the band thing got more and more serious. I still don't know how Pete managed to land us a gig at the Linnanmäki amusement park on its closing day that autumn, but we got to play there for an audience of fourteen thousand. I later heard that people were complaining about the volume from two and a half miles away. It was one of our first real gigs, as we had previously just played some youth clubs in Herttoniemi (and gotten banned for life). Well, we were ready to conquer the world.

"I really hate ya, ya got some problems, I don't care, I just wanna have sex with ya!" Räkä-Malmi screamed his lungs out and I was all over the stage. The crowd didn't know what the hell was going on. This was in '77. Punk had arrived in '76, but it never really hit Finland until that year.

After the gig a guy came backstage and introduced himself: "Hi, my name is Robby Lind." Or was it Lindfors or Lindberg? I think it was Robby Lindberg. Anyway, he was from a label called Finndisc—the guy just had rich parents; he had no idea how to run a label. He knew nothing about music, but we managed to secure a deal with that gig. I had just turned fifteen, and we went to cut our first single soon after.

On the night before entering the studio, we had partied with some cheap wine, and of course we were supposed to load in early in the morning. It was some tiny place in Pitäjänmäki, where all the studios in Helsinki were at the time. We got to work, and the guys started doing the drum sound check. I watched and listened carefully because it was totally a new experience for me. I was like, Wow, here we are in the studio.

The producer was an idiot called Kassu Halonen. I mean, what kind of a producer would say: "Yeah, it doesn't sound good now, but it will be okay later on"? Man, if it doesn't sound right in the first place, why even mix the damn thing? It's supposed to sound good from the get-go!

I had a really good guitar sound, but the producer said there was too much distortion. Fuck him. Well, I listened to that asshole, and the sound on that record is just awful. The lead breaks are okay, if you can even call them leads, because it was just baby stuff back then. We really wanted a raw, live sound.

We had decided to record everything at the same time, but when we were about to start, for some reason my stomach turned upside down. It just went like this dryer, you know, where you dry your clothes. I could feel the bass drum inside my temples. It felt like somebody was pounding my head with a sledgehammer, and then I barfed right on the studio floor. Everybody was like, what the fuck, man! They tried to clean it up a bit, but the puke stank to high heaven. It really made me feel better, though.

Finally our first single was in the can. Everything was recorded in a day and mixed on the following day, but naturally we were no longer welcome in the studio.

At that point we had offended an amusement park crowd of fourteen thousand and puked on the floor of the first studio

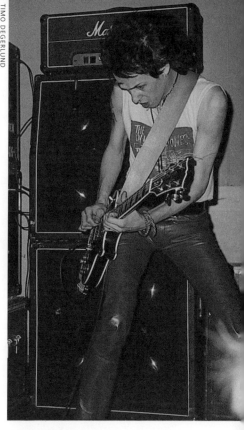

we had ever set our foot in, so basically we could go no further. But we still did, and the single was released. I guess it's kind of a collector's item today among punk collectors. On the back cover you can see Armi Aavikko's breasts, the former Miss Finland from 1977. No, wait, the thing was that Danny and Armi had printed these heart-shaped stickers you could see all around the city, and we made our own heart-shaped sticker that just had fuckin' big tits on it and "Briard" written on top with a magic marker. In East Helsinki you could see them on all the buses and bus stops and shopping malls.

Sometime somewhere, maybe someday someone somewhere will remember.

Briard started to attract a following. We soon learned it was no use playing leftist shindigs, because they didn't pay anything, so we started doing these Conservative Party dances. The pay was good and we got enough beer. We started to recognize familiar faces in the audience, and we were getting pretty fuckin' good.

In those days, for some insane reason, a musician had to be either a politically aware Red or a capitalist. We didn't give a fuck: as long as we got paid. We played anywhere, which usually meant the capitalist hops, because the commies paid jackshit.

Then it was time to do the second single, and we were booked in the legendary Microvox studio in Lahti. A lot of classic albums have been made in that toilet, like the debut of Hurriganes, but it really was a goddamn dingy, slimy hole— even the ceiling was so low that you had to walk half-crouched. The walls were covered with crude pieces of felt to make it soundproof. "Fuck the Army" was recorded there. The flip side has "Product of the TV Generation," one of Briard's best tracks, in my opinion.

After that I started hanging out in Stockholm. I was in Paris for a time, lived in Christiania, Gothenburg, all over Europe, but basically Stockholm was the base where I always returned. Mike came there all the time, too. He had made friends with Jeppe, and we started talking about forming this perfect band.

Okay, I returned to Finland, and all of a sudden I was simultaneously asked to play in two bands: Pave Maijanen's Mistakes, which I guess was one huge fuckin' mistake, and Pelle

MARIA VÄST

Young Pelle (before dreadlocks) and an even younger Sami + me.

Miljoona. I talked to Atte Blom and he said: "Of course you should join Pelle Miljoona—what would you do with those old farts? Especially because Pelle could break big any time, if he'd just get the right band behind him." Well, I joined Pelle. We tried to get Makke in as the bassist, too, and Tumppi Varonen was really interested, as he should've been, too. Makkonen practiced till blood spurted out his fingertips, and in the end, he was very impressive, but Ari Taskinen voted for Sami, and because of that, I didn't like Sami at all for the first three months.

I still remember how we drove to my first gig with Pelle Miljoona. We had some fuckin' lunatic from Tampere driving us, this real crackpot, and the window of the bus was broken. It was -13°F outside, and I sat there wrapped in a blanket and wondered, like, "What the fuck, is this what it means to play in a successful rock band?" But then we got back home and got something like $150 each, and it was so fuckin' cool, because I had never gotten that kind of money for a single gig.

We did some gigs here and there and kept on rehearsing and writing new tunes. I guess the first one was "Olen Kaunis"—no, I really don't remember, but anyway, we went to record *Moottoritie on kuuma*. There was a great vibe in the studio and everything came together really spontaneously. We should've known that the album was gonna be a runaway success. Back then, Taskinen was on a roll. He could write these great pop songs, and there's stuff on that album that's so good it's unbelievable. When I listen to *Moottoritie on kuuma* today, it still sounds as fresh as on the day it was recorded.

Okay, we cut the LP, and next we were supposed to tour

Lapland. Two days before the tour Taskinen started looking for me. At that point, me and Mike had decided to leave for Stockholm and start Hanoi Rocks.

One problem was that Nasse had no guitar gear, because we had sold his amp to get the money for the boat tickets. It so happened that I knew how to get into Pelle's rehearsal space, and one day Makke and Sami broke in through the roof. They just told everyone that they had forgotten the keys. Sami's dad was driving, and he had no idea what the guys were up to. He just thought that they had forgotten their keys. They hauled away

So who's a yuppie, then? Get a load of this fuckin' picture! Andy, the boy next door, with Ralf Örn. Maukka Perusjätkä was already an idea in his head—he just had to find the Maukka.

JUHA HÄMÄLÄINEN

Stefu's—Stefan Piesnack's—amp and stuff, and that became Nasse's guitar gear.

I later heard that they had been driving for a couple of hundred yards when the cops pulled them over. Makke broke into a sweat like, "Oh shit, now we're fucked!" But the cops just said, "Hey, the other taillight is broken, you should fix it." Sami's dad knew nothing, so he just thanked the cops and promised to take care of it. Mike and Sami were just shitting their pants. As usual, I had just planned the heist and was not present myself. Well, the crime's already expired—it's been like twenty-five years.

So we packed our gear and traveled to Stockholm. Jeppe had found us a rehearsal place, and we began practicing like crazy. I called Sami, who had just returned from London, and told him to get his ass to Stockholm, because I'd gotten this band going. "Where can I sleep?" he asked. "We have a place to stay, it's all taken care of," I said. Sami arrived, and in two days we had spent all his money.

The rehearsal place was at the Universiteten underground station. We had to sleep there pretty often, because we couldn't get out between 1:30 and 5:30 AM, when the front entrance was locked. It was fuckin' damp and cold as shit in the winter and really hot in the summer, but there we rehearsed. Makke had already met Seppo Vesterinen earlier and introduced him to me. Seppo decided to be our manager, and we just thought we'd see what would happen next.

ALL THE YOUNG PUNKS

from Hilse 3/80

ELI
ANDY MONROE
KERTOILEE IT-
SESTÄÄN, SUO-
MENMAASTA,
RUOTSISTA JA
MUSIIKISTA

STORY BY
ZEUS MATTILA

Andy Monroe
Tells About Him-
self, Finland,
Sweden, and Music

Story by
Zeus Mattila

I just found this somewhere. The names might be confusing because
the interview was done right before we divvied up the names in the
band. Try and make some sense of it—it's basically just a young gun
shooting his mouth off.
It's only punk rock but I ♥ it!

What kind of a guy is Antti "Andy McCoy / Monroe / Von Hulkko" Hulkko? At least he has a slew of names, like all beloved children should. Not that Andy would be a child—totally the opposite.

Be that as it may, he tells about himself in the following story, answering some of your questions, leaving some unanswered, and raising some new ones. Take it away, Andy, the fuse is burning.

YOU SHOULD DIE WHEN YOU FEEL OLD...

My horoscope sign is Libra and I play guitar. My hair is originally dark brown but at the moment it's multicolored. I have four piercings in one ear and one in the other. I like beer and pot, some girls are okay, some are not. I like nice clothes but I don't like rubes and hicks. And I don't mean people who live in the sticks, because there are rubes everywhere. A rube is a rube. I formed my first band in Stockholm. None of us knew how to play. I had practiced with a nylon-

stringed acoustic guitar. I didn't listen to any records at the time, so we just played our own stuff. Then I came to Finland. To my misfortune I met Pete "Räkä" Malmi, and we formed Briard. I did a couple of gigs and a few singles with them but then I realized it wasn't my thing. Because each time we made a record Pete always said there was something wrong with the covers because all my songs had been credited to Pete. I went to ask the label bosses and they said that

3-vuotias tyttö vailla PÄIVÄ-HOITAJAA väliltä Kauriala—keskusta. kuun alusta alkaen. Vast. p

Pete had told 'em they were his songs. Stuff like that. Then I returned to Stockholm and I had a band called Nymphomaniac, but the guy who was supposed to buy the PA traded the equipment for a sailboat. I returned to Finland for a while but went back to Stockholm pretty soon. I played in various lineups but then I formed a trio called Pain. It was a killer band. This country has never seen a band like that. We split up because our bass player did too much junk because you can get it so easily in Stockholm. Then I came back to Finland and Taskinen asked me if I wanted to join a new band they were planning

with Pelle. I said okay, whatever, a band is a band.

PUNK IS DEAD BUT WE'RE STILL DYING...

Okay, actually I knew Ari Taskinen before all that. We had often jammed together back in '78–79, and it felt good to play in a band again. Okay, then I met Sami, who hadn't even heard the first album by the Clash at the time. Well, I played it for him and now he digs the Clash, too. We've so far done, dunno, maybe twenty gigs, and it's all coming together. I think our overall sound has really changed since we started, and it will change even

26

more, and that will come as a surprise to many people. I used to play different stuff in the beginning, more complicated stuff, but then Taskinen asked me to keep it simple so that the music would be more catchy. And of course Taskinen bought that Yamaha keyboard that cost $2,200. He already had that at the Kaivopuisto gig. So surely our sound continues to evolve. We did a tour of Lapland, two weeks and something like eleven gigs, and I think it was ridiculously short. I guess I'm not like the other guys, because I could have just continued like a year or so. I only got into touring mode on the second to last gig, and shit, it was a real bummer to know that the day after next we would be back in Helsinki. The others thought it was cool to get back home, but I would have liked to go on. Kolari was the northernmost place we played. It's close to the Swedish border, and there were a couple of Swedish girls there who wondered what I was doing in Finland because I spoke such good Swedish. And punk was surprisingly popular up there. There were quite a few punks around. Yeah, although our sound is changing, my own songs don't really fit in yet, but we shall see. I think the songs by Pelle and the others are pretty cool anyway.

STOCKHOLM IS A BIG CITY COMPARED TO HELSINKI...

I think Stockholm is better than Helsinki in all respects. There are better chicks in Stockholm, it's easier to get dope, and that's where I met Anna, who's still my girlfriend, although I have other girls, too. In Stockholm I was mostly a bum, although I did some odd jobs, like cleaning, laundry, whatever. Oh yeah, for a while I also ran a horse-betting racket at Solvalla. That's a racetrack. I had no other property except my guitars. I walked around in the same unwashed jeans for four months and washed my hair every three months. I had a natural Sid Vicious look though my hair was longer.

All of my old friends live in Stockholm. I actually know Stockholm better than Helsinki. I still sometimes get lost here.

HANOI ROCKS IS THE COOLEST BAND IN FINLAND

I think Hanoi Rocks is the best band in Finland. There's two really killer guys in the band. There's nothing like Hanoi Rocks anywhere in the world, and in a year it will be even more killer. It's either going to top the charts, or at least it's going to be one hell of a cult band. I also listen to the Widows. I think T. B. Widow is a true punk rocker.
The punks out at the condemned wooden houses in Kallio, or Kill City, really kick-started the scene, and I think it was a really cool thing. I'm a good friend of Maukka Perusjätkä, the new wave star, and I've often jammed with those guys. I was originally meant to play on that Säpinää LP, but then I got bored and went back to Stockholm to smoke pot. If I had been on that LP, it wouldn't have turned out so shitty. Jimi Sumén is also a good friend of mine, although I don't necessarily like everything he does these days. But as a person he's great.
I remember when Jimi became famous after a gig at Kultsa, and this hippie complained to me how he

could play the same stuff
too. A copy is a copy, but
I still think nobody has
played Hendrix songs better
than Jimi. These hippies
could never do that, because
Hendrix demands sex and
aggression, and they have
none whatsoever.

A COLD BEER IS A GOOD FEELING

I think it's stupid to ask
whether somebody prefers
drugs or alcohol because
you can't really compare
them. Sometimes a cold beer
is the best thing I can
think of, but sometimes beer
just doesn't hit the spot.
There's different music for
different moods, too.
I like Kiss, Foreigner,
AC/DC, Aerosmith, and R.E.O.
Speedwagon. Some say they're
heavy metal but I don't
think so. They're just good
rock 'n' roll bands. I don't
like metal stuff like Black
Sabbath, Purple, and so on.
And I also hate prog bands.
I like the basic punk stuff:
Pistols, Clash, Buzzcocks,
X-Ray Spex, Boys, Criminals,
and Destroy All Monsters.
I recommend Destroy All
Monsters to everybody who
digs good music. Then
there's obviously Ramones
and Dolls. But bands such as
Angelic Upstarts and Cockney
Rejects are bullshit. Those
guys don't have a clue what
punk is. I think they're
more like all these James
Dean kids hanging around in
Helsinki—they can't even

play.
There's not a whole lot
of guys around who can
really play. I think the
best guitarist in Finland
is Nasse McCoy, and then
there's J. B. Hutto, the
legendary American blues
guitarist, a true virtuoso
of slide guitar. Chuck Berry
is also an idol of mine.
He's played the same solo
for twenty-five years, but
that solo is so great it's
insane. Then there's Link
Wray and the late Stones
guitarist Brian Jones. Those
are the most important.

MONEY IS THE BEST INVENTION THAT'S BEEN INVENTED...

Yeah, you can buy everything
with money: women, booze,
whatever you want. Being
anticommercial is a
cliché. There simply are

no noncommercial bands. If
I record a noncommercial
record, for example, it
will become commercial as
soon as some idiot buys it.
The other thing that pisses
me off is when somebody
claims to be the first to do
something, like somebody
claims he was the first punk
in Finland. Nobody's ever
first in anything, there's
always others doing the
same thing at the same time.
Guys like Eurovision soul
singer Timo Kojo and singer-
songwriter Dave Isokynä
Lindholm may say certain
things about me, but they
are just clones themselves.
Kojo is Finland's leading
Rod Stewart clone, and
Isokynä is the biggest Bob
Dylan clone.

sinpentuja

524.

DESTROY YOURSELF!

I haven't spent much time in school. I just did the obligatory stuff and a couple of years of art school in Stockholm. There were some nice chicks there but I bailed out when they started pulling this Picasso shit. My artful interests include reading comics like Donald Duck, the Phantom, and Katzenjammer Kids, and seeing good horror and catastrophe movies like <u>Halloween</u>, <u>Clockwork Orange</u>—one of my all-time faves—and a flick called <u>Full Circle</u>. I can't remember the Finnish title. I'm not gonna do anything for my future. I'm just gonna hang out. Maybe one day I'll be in a helluva mess, but that's then and this is now. I'm gonna record a solo single pretty soon, "Kill City Kills"/"I Want You," and nobody's heard anything like that in Finland before. In general, I don't think it's important to have a message in the songs, because if you have a bad song with good lyrics and a good song with bad lyrics, 90 percent of the people will pick the one with the bad lyrics because it's better musically.
I concentrate mainly on the music. That's what's important to me, and that's why I have three guitars: an Explorer, a Gibson Les Paul, and a Flying V.
Playing music is my life. It's neither work nor play, it's my life.
Finally I'd like to thank the following people: Grönberg, Luuka Pekka, Jimi Sumen, Hanna (I love you all).

~ II ~

JAMLO SARISALMI

The first time Vesterinen came to check out our rehearsals, his jaw dropped to the ground. We had practiced so much it was insane. Then we somehow got a place to sleep. Anna, my girlfriend at the time, her father got us an apartment with three rooms and a kitchen. We each had our own room. Well, I guess Sami and Nasse shared a room. Makke spent a lot of time with his girlfriend at the time, Coo Coo. (It was not intimate—basically they were just friends.) That's when he really started shooting up speed. It was fucked, he got so addicted to that shit that once before a rehearsal I said that if he didn't get his act together, he'd be out of the band. But in my condition, who was I to pass judgment on anybody? A young buck is a young buck. I later did that myself for years, but I don't need that shit no more. In those days, you really could've kicked Mike out, but later it would've been impossible,

32

— SHERIFF —

because Mike had become such an integral part of the band and also my best friend. We kept on rehearsing, and Seppo came to visit us more and more until he finally said that we were ready to cut an LP.

We went to record *Bangkok Shocks Saigon Shakes Hanoi Rocks* right away, and that album surprised everybody in Finland. The critics were dumbfounded how Andy could have pulled off something like that, because they had just written me off as some fuckin' loony, although I've always planned and realized my stuff really methodically. Then we did the longest tour in the history of Finnish rock 'n' roll. I think we still hold the record: fifty-eight gigs in fifty-six days, or was it fifty-nine? We played every goddamn nook and cranny in this country. Ay, ay, ay! We started to build a following and saw that people were hitchhiking

One of the first Hanoi Rocks photo sessions.

MOSES

to our gigs. It just got bigger and bigger. After the tours, we used to go back to Stockholm and return to play gigs during the weekends. After a while we figured it was time to move to the U.K., as it was the only way to break big internationally. These were all McCoy/Monroe decisions, as the two of us still used to decide everything.

I still remember our first gig in the U.K. There were six people and a three-legged dog in the audience. I thought it was actually pretty good—at least somebody came. Hey, you gotta start from the bottom. In just a couple months, the clubs were packed. This all coincided with the recording of *Oriental Beat*.

I gotta slip in a story about our rehearsals in Stockholm. We had just moved into a real rehearsal studio with a proper P.A. and all the goods to rehearse for the album. Seppo came in one day and told us that Helge, who was our first roadie and a

JAMLO SARISALMI

guy who really believed in us—a true *calo*—had hung himself. I had just met him a couple of weeks earlier on Kasarmintori, Helsinki, and he had his girlfriend with him and seemed real happy. Then I heard the sad news. Helge never got to share the success we achieved later on, although he had been with us since day one. Goddammit, he was there in Virrat on fuckin' New Year's Eve 1981, ever since those days. It was real sad.

But yeah, we went to England, recorded an album, played the clubs, and word got around. When we came back for the Finnish summer festivals, we realized we had started a kind of a movement: The crowd either hated us or loved us. And that was just perfect.

Then the U.K. Subs came to Finland, and we had to open up for them. We were still total newcomers. There were all these skinheads in Tampere, and hell, Mike Monroe obviously looks like the ideal Aryan man, so they began throwing darts at us when we played. A horrible fight ensued, and I hit this skinhead on the head with my Les Paul, a guitar that weighs over eleven pounds. The guy's head just popped open like an overripe tomato, and there was blood everywhere. Jeppe lost his temper, jumped over his drums, and attacked some guy with his

Stockholm, after the gig at Studion club in '82.

drumsticks, and there was more blood. It all ended in total chaos. The U.K. Subs loved the show.

Back to the album. It all started when *Sounds,* one of the most popular hard rock mags in the U.K., got a copy of our LP. They sent a guy from England called Dave Roberts to do a piece on us, and we got a full page in *Sounds.* He ranted that we were going to be the biggest sensation since the Stones and the Beatles, you know, the album's incredible, the band looks great, you better watch out. He could already see it. And that really opened doors for us. The press got really interested in us and the gigs got rave reviews. We really gave it everything we had.

All right, we returned to Scandinavia. It was winter and our first gig was in Virrat, a rural place in the middle of Finland. I had gotten into a fight with Anna, my girlfriend, whom Jeppe had known since they were kids. Jeppe got mad and jumped me from behind while I was playing. I think it's even on video.

Then this local fuckin' hick roadie just decided to sit in the middle of the stage while we were playing. I told him to fuck off, because it was our gig and our stage for the time being. I threw a bottle at him, but he wouldn't budge. Fortunately the bottle missed him. Then Jeppe jumped me, and suddenly all the security guys were on top of me too. Of course I grabbed my guitar and smashed two or three guys in the head. Then I ran backstage, locked the door behind me, and just blew my top—

Andy had to let off some steam. I completely destroyed these wall-sized mirrors and everything. Finally Seppo managed to get in to tell me there were sixteen big guys, as big as the doors of the local church, waiting for me outside, like, "Goddamn, we'll take care of the homo from Helsinki! The freak is probably on drugs!"

I hadn't even smoked weed for a month. Oh, you ignorant people. Thou shalt not judge them but pity them. Only Jah can judge. But somehow I got out alive. The guys hid me in the back of the bus because the cops were on their way and I didn't want any trouble.

Later the local security pressed charges. I think I even had to fly back from the Far East to the Virrat courthouse because all these guys, seven big guys, wanted money from me. One guy had a stiff neck; the other was supposedly unable to tend to his fuckin' cows for a week because his back was so sore, I had supposedly beaten them up so bad. In the end, they came up with such ridiculous ailments it was hard to keep a straight face anymore. The judge, who was their good friend—probably bought his moonshine from the guys—was just like, yeah, Andy has to pay damages. None of them even

DREAMS OF A BETTER WORLD • I do dream of a world where people wouldn't spend the money on weapons, the kind of money that would feed all the starving people of the world for five years. I wish that drug addiction and alcoholism were wiped out. I wish the drug problem would go away. There's a medicine for everything, and I wish everybody would find the right way so they wouldn't have to steal or lie. I wish people would find peace deep within themselves, because they can never find it without themselves. The peace is within us all, and we always carry it with us. That's where the innermost peace can be found. And I also wish that there would be no armies, borders, or police, yet people would still be able to live in harmony. But I know I won't see these things happen in my lifetime. And if you're reading this two hundred years from now, I doubt you have seen them, either. But maybe one day—and that's one thing that gives me the strength to continue—maybe I'll be able to see that a tiny part of what I did with my music gave inspiration to people around the world, and these people will keep the flame burning. That flame will always burn somewhere. It will never die. It is the human will to live in balance and love.

had a doctor's certificate. We appealed, and in the end all charges were dropped. Man, you should have some kind of proof if you're asking for money! They just wanted to milk a rock star, a rock star who had just started making some serious money.

So we wrapped up the Finnish tour, and because Jeppe had attacked me, he had to go. That's why he was sacked, plus the fact that his suicide bullshit was getting to me. It's tough when a member of the band becomes depressed, but everything just kept on getting worse and the pressure became too much for him. It was better to relieve him of his duties. I didn't want to be responsible if he killed himself. I said that he would finish the tour and that was it. Jeppe was later in tears saying he was sorry, and that was okay. He's still a good and loyal friend of mine.

I already had another guy in mind. We had met this guy called Razzle in London. We had a vacation coming, and for the first time since we started the band, we had money to go to London to just relax and hang out, so me and Anna flew over. Richard Bishop, who later became the co-manager of Hanoi, was in the States for a month, so we lived in his apartment. On that trip I finally got my first vintage white Les Paul. It was a dream come true, although the guitar basically meowed like a cat in heat. Then when Richard returned, Razzle said we could crash at his place.

We hung out with Razzle, had loads of fun, and became real good friends. We lived in Islington, Northern London, and decided that Raz would come back with us to Scandinavia. We figured we'd start rehearsing in Stockholm to break him in.

There were now three of us, so we didn't have enough

Building up the band somewhere on the road. What do you mean, "Who's singing?"

money for the flights, but luckily we managed to cash in our old plane tickets after a doctor wrote us sick papers. We got £350, bought three train tickets to Stockholm, and left London full of enthusiasm. Razzle especially was bursting with excitement, as it was his first time outside the U.K.

The problems began at the Dutch border: Razzle didn't make it through the passport inspection. Well, I ran back through the customs and said that he was my responsibility. I flashed 'em a wad of cash and told 'em that the guy sure had money, I was just carrying it for him, and that he would be staying as my guest in Stockholm. They were already about to deport him, but finally they let him go.

We had to wait a day in Copenhagen, so I decided to show

Razzle around. We went to Christiania, walked along Ströget, drank Danish beer, smoked Moroccan hash, took it easy. After a couple days we reached Stockholm, where we stayed for a while, and again I showed Razzle around town. He was excited like a little kid, because he had never been outside London. Raz really enjoyed his life, and that's the most important thing.

Then we went to Helsinki. They had booked us a rehearsal studio that we could use during the nights, and after rehearsing for a while we headed straight out for our first tour.

We had a friend with us at the first gig, a guy who's now a doctor of philosophy. He used to get really drunk and come onstage during the last song. This guy was really fat, and he just jumped around naked while we laughed our asses off. He was also responsible for guarding the tour bus, and when Razzle tried to get in, he hit him in the head with a fuckin' baseball bat. Razzle lay there unconscious, and I was like, "What the fuck, man, that's our new drummer!" The guy just said, "Oh, he is, isn't he, sorry about that." And that was it.

A really sad episode took place at the back of the bus that night. There was a chick who the guys took turns fucking; she just kept on asking whose turn it was. This fat guy went and banged her on the head, yelling, "Blow me, you fuckin' whore." I've never seen a guy that big have a pecker that small. It was pitiful. He was the only one the chick didn't want to fuck.

Anyway, we were breaking Razzle's balls. We told him

this would be his trial by fire: He'd have to fuck that girl. Seven or eight guys had already done her, so she was like a total sewer, but Razzle had no problem rising to the occasion. He just stuck his dick in. Yuck! But hey, at least he had become a full-fledged member of the band. Although he would have been that anyway, even if he skipped the so-called trial by fire.

The next day we were playing at some festival, and there was this small pond nearby. Razzle and Sami decided to have a swim, and Nasse didn't need much convincing either. They jumped in with their clothes on, but when they rose from the "water," they were all covered in some pitch-black, oil-like substance and their gear was totally ruined.

We just kept on going. Nasse did speed for a number of days till his liver just gave out one night. Fortunately he had some groupie with him. He had done speed for three, four days, and the weather was in the high 80s. I'd been on the roll myself, but I felt it was about time I hit the sack. We spotted an unlocked boat on the shore and thought about going rowing, but as we only had two bottles of Koskenkorva left, I decided that, hell, I won't be bothered. Nasse went, drank both bottles, and passed out in the heat. Later during the night he just collapsed and started sweating piss. In other words, his liver said no.

It was horrible to visit him in the hospital the next day. We had to put on sterile clothes, and Nasse's blood was circulating through some kind of machine. We played the next gigs without him. On the night when Lita Ford (ex-Runaways) was supposed to open up for us, we only played one song and trashed our gear, because the sound on stage was so crappy. I guess we had already gotten used to better conditions.

41

— M c C o y —

III

We had no expectations whatsoever when we went to the Far East for the first time. We had absolutely no idea how it would be over there. We had just completed a U.K. tour, and the U.K. had been damp, cold, and rainy, typical English weather in the winter. On our first trip to the Orient in January 1983 we were supposed to play Bombay and Delhi in India, and then continue to Hong Kong, Japan, and Thailand. We'd have a one-off in Bangkok, and then we'd wrap up with a vacation in Thailand.

We left London on a cold, rainy day. Everybody was dressed in heavy winter gear because it was so chilly. Fortunately I had been watching BBC World, so I knew the temperature in Bombay was in the high '80s. I'd just forgotten to tell the other guys—I wasn't in the habit of thinking too much about the Fahrenheit or Celsius degrees around the world. In the plane we just drank and slept. I think Razzle got into a fight with some close-minded idiot, and finally we reached Bombay.

At the time, the Indian passport and customs system

was total chaos, the kind of farce that no sane person could even imagine. Fortunately I remembered the difference in weather before we left the plane and changed my clothes. I suggested the others do the same, but their gear was packed in flight cases. Well, I slipped into white jeans and a loose white shirt, and I was in luck. As soon as they opened the plane door in Bombay, a horrible stench hit us in the face, the kind of stink that

Outside a girls' school in Bombay.

you can't find even in the sewers of the Western world, and simultaneously a big wall of heat rolled over us. It was like somebody hit you in the head with a hammer. And then it was time for the drama that was the passport and customs inspection. It lasted for something like four and a half hours. There was no line whatsoever; people just elbowed each other. The other guys were sweating like pigs and wondering what kind of a fuckin' UFO planet we had landed on. Well, I was wondering just about the same thing.

An Indian promoter was there to meet us. Only one major Western rock band had played in India before us, the Boomtown Rats, Bob Geldof's first and last successful band, but they had only played Delhi. The Police and Sting came after us. It was a new experience both for us and the Indians.

They had scheduled four days off for us to shake the jet lag and get accustomed to the climate. We arrived at the hotel at something like three or four in the morning. When I got into my room, I saw three twenty-inch lizards on the wall. I totally freaked out and ran to reception. Everybody else was there too, and we were pretty fuckin' upset: "Hey, there's some creatures climbing on the walls! Horrible lizards! Are they dangerous? What are they doing in my room?"

This guy at reception tried to calm us down: "No, no, sir, they're nice animals—they eat the insects. This way bugs won't bother you; they might not come in at all." Bombay is built on ancient swampland, and without the lizards, apparently the rooms would be filled with all kinds of mosquitoes and insects.

HANOI IN JAPAN • First time in Japan, there was already some hysteria in the air. We could never have imagined how it would be the next time, because it was ten times more intense. But hey, Hanoi was Hanoi, and I'll never forget how it was.

And the beggars, oh man, there were more bugs on them that I had ever seen in my life. We were outside the hotel, drinking gin from the bottle, and it didn't take long till we were surrounded by seven, eight guys, all kinds of local people. Night people, homeless people, yuppies on their way home from the disco, diseased cripples—and me, Sami, and Razzle. Of course I passed the bottle, as I thought it would be a good way to learn about the local mentality. The bottle went round and round, from me to Razzle, from Razzle to the seven diseased Indians, and back to Sami. After a couple of rounds, Sami realized it and went fuckin' berserk.

"You asshole! You give me the bottle after all those diseased people have drunk from it! What the fuck! I could get leprosy, or worse!"

Well, who gives a shit. We emptied the bottle, got nicely drunk, and decided to go check out the surroundings as the sun was rising. Sami and I walked to Gateway of India, located right next to the hotel. It's a place where the Portuguese first set foot on mainland India sometime in the fifteenth or sixteenth century. I guess that's where the name comes from. We thought we'd take a boat ride to an island off Bombay where they take the dead. The lowest caste, or one of the lowest castes, work there, the "untouchables." They crush the skulls, bones, and internal organs of the dead, and vultures dine on what's left. The closer we got to the island, the more unbearable the stench was. About a mile away the stink was already so sickening that we had to throw up. There was no option but to turn back.

Okay, it was so hot that Sami and I thought that what the fuck, we'll just cool our feet in the water. As soon as we'd dipped our feet in, the locals started yelling: "Feet up! Feet up!" We wondered what they meant, because Seppo had explained to us all about the local customs, what you could do and what you shouldn't do to not offend the local religious practices. We thought that maybe it was some kind of a religious thing, something that was taboo to one of those thousands of sects. We were just like, "Would you shut up, please, just let us cool our feet in the water because it's so fuckin' hot." They were like, "No, no, this is not religious, look, look!" Then we saw this shark, a shark fin: Three or four sharks were swimming probably sixteen feet from us. They were circling around us and kept getting closer and closer. Fuck, we had our feet up in a quarter of a second like in a sped-up film. The guy told us that a shark had really bitten a tourist in the leg and pulled him into the water, and a pack of sharks had instantly devoured him.

We returned to the harbor and saw there was some kind of a battleship anchored there. We had this crazy photographer with us, Justin Thomas, who had become our personal lensman. Justin started snapping pictures of Sami and me because he

thought the battleship made such a great backdrop. They started yelling at us from the ship and even shot in the air a couple of times, and once again we were warned: "Don't do that, don't photograph the battleship, they can shoot you!" He told us that the soldiers had shot some tourists who had taken pictures. This was India back in 1983. We realized we were in a different world altogether.

Later, we decided to score some hash with Sami and make everyone happy. We thought we would have no trouble finding some, because that's where the goddamn stuff

Andy and Gretsch.

was made, after all. We checked out some cabs till we found a guy who looked promising. The driver was instantly like, "Oh, *charas!*" That's the local name for hash. "Yes, yes, I can get, I get anything you want. Get in my cab. You gentleman, me friend, I show you Bombay."

The cabbie kept on driving for twenty minutes through side streets and back alleys, and soon we realized there was no way we would find our way back by ourselves. Me and Sami started to get a bit worried when the guy picked up his friend along the way, getting afraid that they might mug us. More minutes passed as the cabbie kept on driving through dark alleys. Finally I gave him twenty English pounds and told him to get some hash for us, as much as he could get for that money. The cabbie disappeared into this house and lingered there for a long time. We waited and waited. Then the guy returned and threw the load into my arms. "Here you go." I had both hands full of the stuff: a fuckin' fifteen-gram lump of hash, ten grams of opium, five grams of brown smack, and five grams of white smack. He even gave some comps, like, if you want more, look me up, my name is so and so, whatever. Can't remember anymore.

I instantly told Sami to hold the stuff. He didn't even realize at first, but then it dawned on him: "Fuck, what if we get stopped with this load? Asshole, you just shoved everything to me!" The cabbie drove us back to the hotel and tried to sell us everything from hookers to gold. We politely refused.

We got back to our room. Everybody was chilling out with cold beer and drinks, and naturally our surprise souvenir was warmly welcomed. Some serious smoking ensued. I was puffing, Nasse was probably smoking the brown heroin, and we all ate opium and smoked hash. They told me I turned all blue, so I thought that maybe it was time to fuckin' chill out, and I went back to my room with Sami. We were pretty tired because we hadn't slept since the plane landed in Bombay.

Well, we were both nodding and fell into a deep slumber. I finally woke up to a persistent knock on the door. This guy just wouldn't give up, and the banging continued with increasing fervor. Sami was lying on the floor, and I told him to go see who it was. He told me to do it myself, he was too tired. Well, I got up and went to the door. My head felt like it was made of lead, and my body seemed to weigh a ton. I opened the door, and a guy gave me a note. I don't know how he got inside the hotel, because they had pretty tight security. There was something written in Hindi on the note, and I was like, "Hey, I don't understand, me panjara, in English, sir, please." The note said: "Help me out financially. I can't support myself because my parents cut off my tongue as a child so it would be easier for me to beg."

Then he opened his mouth. There was just a stump where the tongue had been. I almost got sick and slammed the door shut. I went back to bed, and just when I was about to fall asleep again, I heard it again: THUMP! THUMP! I told Sami to get the fuck up because it was his turn, but he just couldn't move. I guess he felt like his whole body was made of lead too. I went to the door, but there was no one there. At this point I didn't even remember I was in India anymore. I was neither awake nor asleep. Once again I heard the knocking, yet there was nobody behind the door.

— SHERIFF —

A band that became larger than life.

The knocking continued. I was thinking it must be the cleaning lady. We must be in some hotel in the States and our room's on ground level. That's how the cleaning ladies get in. I open the curtains and I see a baby floating in midair. Our room was on the third or fourth floor. I thought I was about to go crazy, that the Hesperia loony bin already had a padded cell waiting for me but maybe a little too late. I asked Sami: "Do you see what I see, or have I lost it?"

Sami raised his head sleepily: "What?" If you had seen the look on his face, you'd understand how sick the whole situation was. In two seconds he was wide awake and screaming by the window: "That fucking thing is floating in the air!" We opened the window and saw some old crone below balancing a long stick on her forehead.

She had tied the baby to the stick. At the same time she was hustling tourists, the baby was begging through the hotel windows. That was pretty sick. Although probably very profitable, if you look at it from their angle.

After waking up, we decided to see what the others were up to. I went to Nasse's room. Nasse and Razzle shared a suite. I knocked. There was no answer for a small eternity. Then I heard a weird sound from the room. CRASH! BANG! FUCK! It sounded like somebody was falling all over the place, crashing into the walls and who knows what else. Finally, after waiting something like twenty minutes, somebody reached the door and opened it. A shirtless Nasse stood in front of me, his body covered with deep, bloody scratches. It looked fuckin' serious. I was like, "Shit, man, how can you let anybody do that to you? It doesn't matter how good-looking the chick is, that's fuckin' painful!" Nasse mumbled sleepily: "It was no fuckin' chick. It's the motherfuckin' opium that makes me itch." When you do opium, you get this urge to scratch yourself and you feel almost no pain at all. Nasse had scratched himself raw. Well, I went downstairs, Sami came too, and we found Richard, Seppo, and the local promoter at the cafe.

"Where the fuck you been?" they asked.

"What do you mean?" I wondered. "We just slept the night. Took it real easy."

They said: "Shit, you've been gone for three days!"

It was a trip to hear we had slept for three days. But hey, at least we felt good. This was before any of us had developed a serious habit. It was basically just headache, if you can call the feeling of having lead in your head an "ache." Mostly it just made you numb.

WE WENT TO CHECK OUT THE VENUE. Rhang Bavan was an auditorium with a capacity of five to seven thousand. After soundcheck, the local promoter asked me how long we would play. I told him that the set usually lasted about ninety minutes, maybe 105 minutes. I guess we had just released our second album—no, it probably wasn't even out by that time. We didn't have the material that we had during the last days of Hanoi, when we were really on fire and 150-minute gigs became the norm, not counting encores. "Goddammit," he said. "No, no, it will be chaos, the crowd will go berserk." We asked why. "Well, the local bands play for seven hours." Seven hours? Like, what the hell, man! Well, we finally managed to scrape up a pretty lengthy set. We would just stretch each song as much as possible.

In the end, the gig lasted about four and a half hours, nonstop. We had a drum solo, a guitar solo—I pulled this twenty-minute solo that had everything: flamenco, slide, blues, widdly-widdly, this and that, even a Celtic sword dance. The crowd went apeshit. We played each song we'd ever recorded, rehearsed, or jammed, right down to old blues standards. Fuck, we probably even did "House of the Rising Sun." The first and hopefully the last time I had to play that song.

When we really got going, the crowd began to dance, and the cops began to beat up people. This was toward the end of the set, as we had built it so that it just grew more intense. Songs just kept getting faster and faster, and in the end, it was just full blast, "One, two, three, go! DUH-DUH-DUH-DUH-DUH-DUH!" A real machine-gun groove. It got really bloody in the end, when the crowd began throwing rocks at the cops.

We left the stage pretty quickly after blood started to flow. We ran backstage, and there was a narrow window, maybe eight inches wide, six-and-a-half feet high, basically just for ventilation. As we peeked through that window, we saw a terrible riot unfold. The cops were beating people mercilessly. The next day we made the front page of the *Indian Times*: "Rock band causes a riot." How did we do that—by playing blues? Suddenly it was our fault, although it was the cops who'd screwed it up.

After the gig, we went to a local disco, where people danced like there was no tomorrow. This was when Culture Club had the hit "Do You Really Want to Hurt Me?" I noticed for the first time that it was a hit in India, too, like everywhere around the world, and I realized that, fuck, an international hit is really an international hit. People are not listening to it in just Europe, the USA, and maybe Japan, like I had previously thought.

From Bombay we flew to Delhi. Delhi was a bit cooler and cleaner than Bombay. The Indian promoter traveled with us, and we got a really nice reception there. We were supposed to play a university auditorium. The first gig in Bombay had been in an open-air auditorium, but this was indoors.

We played a lengthy set once again, and it's a gig I will never forget, because it just went so fuckin' good. We began to understand how you should perform for the Indians—or at least we were a bit wiser than on our first gig over there.

One guy came to our mixer and said that the music was really crazy. "Indian music gets me here," he said, pointing to his head, "but this music hits me here," pointing to his genitals. Awesome.

We still had some hash left from our shopping trip in Bombay, and Mike had also bought—or somebody had given him—some Nepalese Temple Balls. It's the stuff that sadhus use, the holy wanderers of India who only possess the clothes on their back and a small bowl for eating. Temple Balls are their specialty, about the best hash you can get. They smoke it in order to be closer to the so-called god. According to the *Bhagavad Gita*, the Hindu holy book, Shiva smokes bhang day and night, so no wonder his followers do the same. And we were on a pilgrimage, too, after all.

RIGHT BEFORE WE LEFT DELHI, the first of us got sick. Our roadie Spede suddenly just collapsed and lost consciousness. We had expected minor stuff, but this looked serious. Spede had gotten some kind of virus from food or drink. He made it to the plane, but he was real sick.

Mike and I were wondering what to do with the hash. We had never carried anything through customs ourselves, so with a young buck's logic we decided that what the hell, we'd just eat it all—and fuckin' A, on the plane it hit home. First we just totally dropped and fell asleep. Mike and I slept all the way to Hong Kong, and we were still totally spaced when we woke up. We were in some kind of surreal stupor, and we still had to play a gig that night. The next day would be off.

Hong Kong airport was operated like any Western airport. But man, in the city, there was just so much stuff built on this tiny patch of land. In certain parts of the town they came

JUSTIN THOMAS

to sell you everything imaginable. Heroin was so cheap that they just put it in cigarettes. I was too tired to pay any attention. I just went to my room, passed out, and slept like a baby.

In the evening we were taken to dinner, and that food was so good, I just had to keep on eating. Every once in a while I had to go puke because I was so full, and then I just kept on eating. No kidding. Of course cannabis was partly to blame, because it increases appetite like crazy. That's why it's the perfect medicine for anorexics and bulimics, but obviously I was neither. I was just so stoned and the food tasted so damn good.

The Hong Kong show was a club gig in a one-thousand-capacity venue. The crowd was fuckin' great. Mike and I were sitting backstage before the gig—the others were somewhere else—and I asked him, "How're you holding up?"

"I'm still totally fuckin' out of it," he said. "How about you?"

"Same thing, and it's been over twenty-four hours." We were stoned as shit and there was no end in sight.

When Mike and I sat there face to face in Hong Kong after God knows how many Temple Balls, I realized how close we had become. We couldn't talk to anybody about it, not even the other guys—I mean, the leaders of the band were so fuckin' wasted that they were not sure if they could pull off the show. I remember asking Mike if he thought he could make it. He couldn't answer. I said that I wasn't sure if I even remembered how to play anymore. But when we stepped in front of the crowd, fuckin' A, all hell broke loose. People were bouncing off walls and we sweated out the cannabis overdose. When we came back from the stage, we felt almost normal again. Of course we were both still floating in a bad way, as if we had been walking on water. But the water carried our weight. It offered no balance but it did give some support. It was like some kinda gel.

The vibe on stage had been soaking wet, just like in Bombay. It felt as if we had gone swimming with our clothes on, with my fuckin' leather pants and all that crap. Anything to look good on stage.

Yeah, the next day we went to check out Hong Kong. We were warned not to buy anything in the harbor, as you can easily get food poisoning because the local bacteria is so different. Your body has to slowly adapt to it, which usually takes a couple of months. We'd been there for two days. But man, if you'd just seen those giant garlic prawns! They smelled so good that in the end, I was like, what the fuck, I gotta have some. Everybody there was eating them anyway. I didn't get sick right away, and the next day we flew to Japan.

On our first night in Japan we went to this club called the Lexington Queen, a sort of "in" club frequented by all the Western bands and models who had landed a gig in Japan. David Coverdale from Deep Purple happened to be there, and Razzle set his hair on fire. David seemed to think he was the center of the fuckin' universe, and I guess Razzle thought somebody should give him a lesson. A reminder of his mortality. Man, I laughed so hard! There was a big fight, because all the girls who had been sitting with them suddenly left and came to us, even after Razzle had burnt Coverdale's hair. I guess we were better-looking—well, guys in their twenties usually look better than fifty-year-old geezers.

I fell asleep in some corner of the bar. When I woke up, the others had disappeared. I didn't even know the name of our hotel, and I had no idea where I was. Fortunately I found this model chick I had been talking to earlier. (She later became my girlfriend, but more about that later.) We went to her apartment, and she started systematically calling all the good hotels in town until she found the right one. The others had been scared shitless, since it was already morning and there was still no sign of me. I took a cab to the hotel, and the interviews started right away.

I was doing my thirteenth or was it twelfth interview— obviously there had been some photo shoots and whatnot in between—and suddenly I started to feel really heavy. It felt as of somebody had hit me in the head with a sledgehammer. Then everything went black, and I passed out in the middle of an interview. I woke up when somebody was pouring cold water on my face, and then I was helped to my hotel room. I had a horrible fever, almost 104°F. That was the revenge of the king prawns of Hong Kong. I guess I shouldn't have eaten 'em after all. They were really good, but not worth that kind of an ordeal. I just puked and sweated and slept for something like three days.

This girl Justina was with me in the hotel room and took care of me night and day, brought me juice and everything, and I'll always be grateful to her for that. On the third day we had a gig, but I still had a fever. The doctor gave me a shot, some kind of a vitamin cocktail to give me energy for the show. We played Japan for the first time, and I was feeling so fuckin' sick I could barely move. I could just about handle playing guitar, but

I simply had no strength to do the backing vocals. Next day we had off, and I finally began to feel normal again.

The rest of the Japanese gigs went really well. We had no idea how big we were in Japan—we already had a pretty good following in the U.K., but this was something else. There were probably a hundred chicks thronging the hotel lobby, groupies all on a silver platter, but we were warned to steer right clear of them. Brian Setzer from the Stray Cats had recently gotten into a lot of trouble and had had to leave the country because the girl had been underage. Some of these chicks looked twenty but were actually just fourteen. And hey, nobody asks for an ID card when you're about to, you know, do the usual thing. Use your imagination.

FRUIT • Dope in general is often glamorized. And for some reason, forbidden fruit always tastes better when it's forbidden.

There's a magazine called *The Groupie* in Japan. The writers bed rock stars and write reviews of their abilities and attributes. I guess Nasse got pretty good points, because he was later on the cover. I wound up being featured in that mag a couple of years later, and I got full points for size and performance. The craziest thing is that you can find the mag on each fuckin' newsstand over there.

Our first Japanese tour was a great success, and after that we knew we had laid down the groundwork. Next time everything would be so much bigger. On the first tour, we played two- to three-thousand-seaters. On the second tour it just grew and grew.

Thailand, first time in the Far East.

WE ARRIVED IN THAILAND AND HAD A PARTY THE FIRST NIGHT. I had met a guy called Richard Diran in Osaka. He was from San Francisco and decided to tag along because he had some business in Thailand. Over the years, Richard became one of my best friends.

So we had a party that night. I remember me and Sami shared a room in the Dusit Than; which was probably the best hotel in the world at the time, or at least one of the best. Sami, hung over as he was, drank water straight from the tap, and that's something you just don't do unless you've gotten accustomed to local water. Well, he got sick as a dog but still managed to play the show. I remembered my own pain during the Hong Kong prawn poisoning, and I really felt bad for the guy that he even had to play in that condition. But we still played the show. We

JUSTIN THOMAS

One Kid Creole and two Cocopuffs, New York.

just shortened the set a bit, and the crowd loved it. The problem was that afterwards we just couldn't go anywhere in Bangkok, because people recognized us instantly.

Something we noticed in Asia was the bootleg business. It was a real smooth operation: A day after the show your stuff could be bought on each street corner. But you really couldn't find Thai bootlegs, I mean music by Thai artists. The attitude was just to pull a fast one on the foreigners, not the homies.

We then went to Pattaya to chill out for a week and a half, that was really nice. One day we thought we'd get something to jazz us up, so we went to the pharmacy and told a bullshit story about how we were working the graveyard shift and needed to stay awake. Like, "Give us some uppers." The druggist showed us this box, and we asked how many we should take if we wanted to stay awake the whole night. "Take two," he told us.

Well, Mike, my new pal Richard, and I bought some and took twelve pills each. About an hour later we felt like we were doing eighty miles an hour. Or more like 120. Naturally, we also passed them around. We definitely didn't push it on anybody, but everybody was just dying to get some of that stuff.

We were all in this hotel suite and it just got fuckin' crazy. Razzle had rented a motorbike, and at some point Nasse decided to borrow it to get some more pills. He was so out of it that when he left, the bike veered from one side to another. We were just waiting for him to crash, but surprisingly he came back in one piece. Seppo was clapping his hands to a Who song and enthused: "Oh man, I've never felt so good in my life! Goddammit, how can you feel so great?!"

It was fun. Richard D. took us to a Thai girl kickboxing match. It was pretty heavy: These chicks were beating the living shit out of each other, and there was blood everywhere. There was also this cobra guy onstage, and all of a sudden the cobra escaped from his hands. Full panic ensued and everybody ran out. We were sitting in a balcony, so we could just watch the chaos. Of course the guy finally managed to catch his cobra.

On our first day in Thailand, we had asked our promoter to get us something to smoke. We were sitting in Seppo's room, Sami, Seppo, and I, when there was a knock on the door. Seppo opened the door. There was a cop standing in the hallway, and he handed over a paper bag full of first-class weed, really powerful stuff. We found out later that they had this arrangement with the cops, as apparently our promoter was also the head of the secret police. That was why a cop brought us the dope. I wish

Hanoi live. Early '80s.

there were more cops like that. Although in a way it was sad that
a cop had to do that, because he's a cop, after all, which makes
the whole thing completely immoral. If the system's so corrupt,
how can it work at all? They throw all these small-time drug
fiends into jail, while the kingpins, like our "promoter"—who
was most probably also involved in heroin smuggling—are left
in peace. The big guys always walk away.

It's the same thing as if you had a kiosk where you sold
Coca-Cola and they shut down your kiosk, while the factory
was still allowed to produce the stuff. I think that unless you get
rid of corruption on all levels, we're never gonna see a change. I
don't dig that in general. It's bullshit, but that's how it was.

After we had smoked the first joint, we ordered some
tea and toast for three. Soon there was a knock on the door.

There was tea and toast for thirty. There were only three of us, but we were so high on Thai weed that we just told 'em to leave the stuff and charge it on the room bill. There were three carts full of that shit. We were so out of it, we were like, what the fuck, man, how are we gonna eat it all? The rest of the time in Thailand we just took it easy and relaxed. Then it was time to return to the U.K. and begin a new tour.

WE WERE SUPPOSED TO START WORK on our next LP after the Asian trip. I had a pretty clear mental picture of what I wanted, but obviously the songs were not ready. It would be our first album with Razzle. I can't remember the working title—something idiotic, as usual.

The album became *Back to Mystery City*. We had achieved the

kind of status that we now had the means to do everything ourselves. We had our own production company, so most of the money came to us.

We rehearsed for a week, two weeks, something like that, and went to the studio. It was somewhere in southern England, I can't even remember the exact location, maybe Hastings. It was a residential studio, so we had our own rooms and catering. The facilities were available twenty-four hours a day. *Back to Mystery City* was recorded there entirely. We also recorded "Taxi Driver" and "Beer and a Cigarette" in another studio, and they were basically part of the same session, although the songs were spread over two LPs, *Self Destruction Blues* and *Back to Mystery City*.

Around the same time, we went to the States for the first time. We just played the East Coast, New York and its surroundings. Everybody knew we were laying down the groundwork, as the whole thing just kept getting bigger in Europe and the U.K.

THE SECOND TIME HANOI WENT TO JAPAN was pure hysteria. It was frightening, actually. You just couldn't leave the hotel room. The fans were so fanatical, and they were all over the place. One morning I woke up around five and sneaked out through the employee entrance, and it was the only time I got to walk alone in Tokyo. We stayed in the Ginza district, and it's not so nice around there. It's basically just a business district, and not the most beautiful part of Japan—but at least I got to see something. It was much harder to get back into the hotel. I was showered with presents and had to write like a thousand fuckin' autographs once again.

We did lots of promotion, I mean TV and magazines, and one incident in particular was pretty frightening. We were scheduled for a surprise appearance at this radio show, and of course the fans realized during the interview that it was live, and they knew where the radio station was. I think this was in Osaka, not Tokyo.

After the interview we took the elevator down and had a beer. We were supposed to return to the hotel in the limo that was parked outside the back door. The building had the kind of lobby that they have in banks and other buildings—the walls were all glass, maybe sixteen feet high and thirty-two feet wide, real thick glass. There were about 350 fans outside, and they just kept on banging the glass. Suddenly there was a horrible explosion. The fans were packed so tight against the glass, that finally the pressure shattered the glass. At the same instant they were on us, and somebody ripped out my earring.

DEATH • You always gotta be one step ahead of death, because one day we'll all kick the bucket, and it could happen in the strangest of places. But in my mind, death is nothing to be afraid of. I've realized that we're just moving on to a different place. Death is the moment that's most akin to birth. I can't think of anything that's more similar. We come from somewhere and then we leave, but I think we've learnt something when it's time to go.

And if we talk about reincarnation, I do believe it happens, but not necessarily for everybody, and sometimes it can take longer, although the time might not seem so long in that dimension where we go after death. But I still believe that some of us return instantly. I've built my life on the belief that we should learn something during our time here. The only mystery for me is why so many children die before they've had the chance to learn anything. I also believe that there's a lesson to be learned. And that's a hard lesson, if your child dies. I bless and pray for all people who have lost their children, amen.

People have ripped out a total of four earrings from both my ears over the years. That's not what I expected when I was a kid, and that's not the reason why I want to play music to people. It's really frightening when somebody tries to harm you physically. The only thing I could think of in Osaka was to get in the limo as soon as possible and just get the fuck out of there. I started running and was at the limo first, and then I realized Michael Monroe had been left behind. We had been doing the interview with him, Seppo, and our interpreter Daphne, who accompanied us each time we were in Japan. These girls just ran over her. She was a pretty small woman.

It was just so sick, because they didn't give two shits if they hurt somebody. They just wanted a piece of us and tried to tear away Mike's and my hair as a souvenir. Well, they only managed to get one of my earrings; the other was ripped off elsewhere about a year later. I wonder if they sometimes forget that the artist is a human being too, because these people didn't seem to think about it at all. I've never had a problem giving an autograph if somebody wants it and asks for it, but hell, my body is my own property; it doesn't belong to anybody else. I think it's pretty offending when fans get so fanatic that they hurt you, or try to invade your private life however they can. There are a lot of these people around.

The Japanese audience is both extremely friendly and fanatic at the same time. I've never heard any kick-ass Japanese rock bands, and the kids mostly seem to idolize Western bands, especially groups with a strong image, makeup, etcetera. I don't know if it all boils down to Kabuki theater tradition or what.

After all, they loved the New York Dolls in Japan, and Hanoi Rocks was massive there too.

There was this weekly TV show in Japan, a really popular program that everybody from kids to grannies watched, and year after year, Hanoi was chosen as the most popular foreign band. It was a pretty big honor. The ratings of the show were unbelievable: I heard that something like 80 percent of the entire Japanese population watched it. When they were filming it, there were something like ten to fifteen thousand people just in the studio. It felt like a real gig, because the vibe was really good. And all of Japan was in front of the TV watching us.

I had a dream.

Everyone was wearing flowers

and smoking them.

JAMLO SARISALMI

~ IV ~

The Razzle memorial gigs Hanoi played at Kultsalla were part of a festival called Europe a Go Go. We were the Finnish part of it, and the show had some three hundred million viewers around Europe. I think it was a suitable tribute to Razzle. He would have appreciated the magnitude.

When I look back on Hanoi, like what could've come of it and what became of it, I'm pretty realistic. It was pretty much a learning curve for me. I learned how the business works and so on—I mean, how it works outside Finland. Here it's often so fuckin' inane, and there are so many rip-off artists and leeches.

Of course I wish that Razzle wouldn't have died, but you can't change the past. And I wouldn't even want to change it. I feel that everything has a meaning and that it was Razzle's time to go—and that Hanoi was meant to split up when we did. On the other hand, I believe that had the managers chosen a different course, Hanoi might still be together. It was just too much to handle when we had to instantly replace Razzle and Sami and go on tour again. We should have been allowed to take a six-month break so that we would've really been able to think about what we wanted to do next. We would have had more time to consider who we wanted to have in the band. But for some reason, we were in a hurry once again. I guess it was because we had to make money, money, and more money.

Sometimes it feels like people worship money. Cash is their god. It makes me really sick, and in a way, it has made me hate money. Okay, you gotta have some in order to live, but it shouldn't be as important as it is these days. People revere money and do anything for it. When you can get somebody whacked by paying some Russian a hundred dollars, there are no values anymore. It's sad, and it hurts me in an awful way.

I wish that kids today wouldn't be materialistic like my parents' generation, like, you gotta have this kind of car, that kind of summer cottage, and blah blah blah. There are some of those idiots in my generation too, I'm sad to say. But at least in Hanoi Rocks we never did anything just for the money. There was so much more behind it. Mike and I formed a band that we would've dug ourselves. Later we became rich, and that was something we never dreamed about in the beginning. Nowadays people ask me how much money we made. How much did we make? A fuckin' lot, I tell you, but we were also very good at spending it, because the money wasn't as important as it seems to be to some of these guys who save every penny they earn and wait for the interest to grow. What if Razzle had done that? What if he had saved all his money? What good would it do him now that he's dead, I ask you?

Some people still say we should've sued Mötley Crüe. We could've asked for $100 million and we would've won. But we decided that we could never measure a guy's life in dollars, a guy who we loved and who was so close to us. That's why we never took the matter to court. Mike and I decided that.

But that vocalist, Vince Neil, who drove the car on the night Razzle died, he got away much too easy. If you take somebody's life—even if just by vehicular manslaughter—you should be punished more harshly. I think he sat in jail just for one night until he was bailed out, and then he was only sentenced to do some social service—or what's it called, community service.

It really shows how "justice" works in the U.S.: You're innocent if you have enough money. You could see it so clearly in the O. J. Simpson case. When you're fighting a matter in court, if you don't have the cash, you don't matter. Then you're appointed a so-called public defender, a free legal representative who doesn't care two shits about you. He just offers you a certain course of action and recommends you take it. He doesn't even tell you what happens if you lose, and that's something that's probably gonna happen. Over there, money really is God.

DURING THE LAST DAYS OF HANOI, I fucked chicks for breakfast, I fucked 'em for dinner, I fucked 'em all night long. According to my guitar roadie Timo Kaltio, who counted 'em, I had fucked about two thousand girls at the time. If they didn't leave instantly, I just called my roadies to come and take 'em away. Pretty often the roadies partied with these girls, too, and some of 'em always got a little something. When I wanted a groupie, I just went and grabbed one. Alternately, I scored hotel waitresses or chicks from nightclubs.

I remember my first gig with Pelle Miljoona was also the first time when a girl came and rubbed her genitals against my knee. I was like, what the fuck! Fuck. Toward the end of Hanoi, Sami and Anna, my teenage sweetheart, started a relationship. Of course I was wise to their affair, but I already had my own thing on the side. At the time I was only interested in heroin and this French-English girl, a top model called Justina. Anna

Mr. Sam Yaffa.

became pregnant with Sami's child and decided to keep it. Shit, the kid would've gotten better genes if she had kept one of mine. But thank God she didn't, actually. Because God is merciful if you truly pray to him, and God was merciful to me. I would have really been too young to be a father at the time.

I met Anna when I was fifteen and she was fourteen. All in all, she was really good to me. When she was with Sami, she cheated on him all the time. I hope she didn't learn it from me. All those years she was together with me, she never betrayed me. I was the one who cheated on her. Usually I just went to a bar, scored a chick, fucked her in the toilet, and that was it, back to the table. It was really rude. So if somebody screwed up that love story, it was Andy. There were all these girls, models for the most part. Some became really successful, some disappeared, and a lot of 'em ended up doing drugs. And you know what happens if you're not able to quit like I did.

I REMEMBER A COUPLE OF THINGS about Hanoi and karma. Take how Razzle died in a car accident. When he was younger, he had been driving drunk and killed someone on the Isle of Wight in southern England. Razzle only mentioned the incident once, but he still felt pretty bad about it after all those years. I don't know if it had been his girlfriend or friend, but he had been convicted and he had done time. I think Razzle's death was preordained by karmic law: He did something to another person and the same thing befell on him. That's pretty normal. But it was still sad to lose a friend.

Another case of fatal attraction was a girl that Sami was going out with. She used to come to our early gigs, this young, beautiful girl with long, blond hair down to her crotch, and a great body. I know that Sami also met her in private.

At some point this girl heard the good word and was converted. After that I could see that Sami began avoiding her. She carried a Bible with her, and kept explaining how she had been told in her prayers that it was God's will that she and Sami get married and have a child. Okay, that's tolerable, but this girl just kept showing up in London, Japan, Canada, and all around the world. I don't know where she got the money to do that. She was just sixteen or seventeen.

The last time I saw her, we were in Toronto, Canada, and Sami had gone to his hotel room. The rooms were booked using fake names, and we had never used those names before. I have no idea how she had found her way to Sami's room, but there she sat, waiting for him. She refused to leave. After coaxing and begging, Sami finally tried dragging her out by her hair. No use. In the end, we had to call the security. After that she just sat in the lobby. Sami was freaking out. We decided to tell her Sami had flown to London. In reality we snuck him out the back door and sent him to New York until the girl disappeared.

The scariest thing was that Lennon was shot on the same day. We had the feeling that anything could have happened if Sami had told her that he wanted nothing to do with a basket case like her—like, get the fuck out of here! That girl could've done something really crazy, maybe gotten a gun and shot Sami and then herself, too. You never know.

I didn't meet too many freaks like that, except maybe for one chick I met in a pub on Kings Road with Nasse. She was beautiful, probably Persian blood, pretty as a picture, tall, with black, Baal olive skin. But she was a nymphomaniac. It was torture to be in bed with her: She wanted to fuck all night long and just wouldn't stop. And shit, when you've come like five or seven times and somebody just wants to continue, it's a big no-no. I said fuck, this is enough. She thought she would make me jealous if she hit on Mike, but I just laughed because I knew that

Mike would just run away. And in this particular case, it really was the smartest thing to do.

Mike was really passive with groupies. I believe he had his reasons, and that's really his choice to make for himself. I think that during the whole time in Hanoi, I only saw him with a groupie once. Like I already said, I kept on banging 'em in the hotels and nightclubs, blah blah blah. Nasse had the habit of getting shit-faced and then grabbing the first girl he saw, like, "C'mon, let's go." Surprisingly, the girls always went. Razzle used to like to chat them up.

Once, the situation became alarming in Japan. A family, I mean father and mother, came looking for their daughter, and of course they found her with Nasse and Razzle. The problem was that she refused to leave. Razzle tried to shove her out while the parents were shouting at her in Japanese that she must leave with them, but the naked girl just wouldn't budge. It was a helluva show. We were lucky that it didn't blow up in our faces. Fortunately, there were no journalists around.

Razzle really dug Japan. It didn't take long till he had found some girl that he'd always meet when he arrived in Tokyo. Afterwards we always saw him with the same girl. But before we embarked on the final U.S. tour, Razzle suddenly got engaged to a real pretty blond girl. I will not mention her name.

When Razzle got killed and we returned to London, the girl accused me of Razzle's death. She cried and yelled at me. Hey, I wonder if it occurred to her that I felt even worse? They were supposed to get married after the tour, but that dream was crushed. I hope she found someone else in her life who took his place. Because some people are never able to let go of the past, you know.

74

V

In the summer of '91 I had broken up with Anastasia and already completely fallen in love with Angela. First we lived at Angela's place, but it was too small for my guitars and me, so we rented this luxury apartment in Los Angeles.

The house had previously belonged to Burt Reynolds, and it had huge, well-groomed gardens and a spectacular view over the San Fernando Valley. Especially at night, when millions of lights were shining below, it looked as if the stars were reflected in the valley. They even made that same chirping sound. It all created a spellbinding, otherworldly atmosphere that almost made you feel that you were in Shangri-la. Of course, on the left side you could see the famous Hollywood Hills. At times it felt like they were embracing us.

We had a genuine fountain in the garden, not one of these fake ones, and in the center was a small waterfall. At least for me, the waterfall was the most beautiful inspiration in our

KIRSI KOSKINEN

I could eat ya.
Andy and Angela, mid-'90s.

courtyard. It gave birth to a small brook that ran down the side of the mountain. Inside in the living room, the visual centerpiece was a huge TV.

There were far too many rooms in that house for an artist couple. It meant more money down the drain, as interior decorators are not cheap, but I can tell you that we started the renovation with our own two hands. We were already familiar with antiques, especially collecting Oriental pieces. That was another thing that started off as a minor hobby but later grew all out of proportion. There was also a washing machine in the house—a great luxury for me. I had gotten used to life on the road, where laundry is always a problem.

I loved to watch my kid Sebastian. He was always playing video games on that giant TV screen. He loved that because the computer characters were almost as big as him. Maybe in his imagination he really was in the game. Sebastian ran back and forth with the game characters in front of the huge screen. Whee! He was tireless. Seb's room was downstairs, and it was just overfilled with toys. All toys were personally chosen by Sebastian. Angela, as the wonderful stepmother, always took Seb out for "pick-what-you-want" tours in big toy stores. Sebastian got whatever he wanted, but Angela kept him in line. She was tough and loving at the same time. There was no shortage of love in our home, but Angela didn't let the little guy think that he had the power and freedom to do whatever he wanted. That was maybe our difference in raising a small kid: I sometimes had difficulty saying no to him, but Angela only had to give him a glance, and order was restored in our house.

CANDY

The Karaoke King!

I mostly occupied myself with trying to get away from the most destructive of drugs—I'm not talking about alcohol but a narcotic substance called heroin. That's when I finally quit smack. It was a painful process that lasted for nine months, but afterwards I was back in my natural state. I didn't even drink and smoked just a couple cigarettes a day—that was my only vice. I felt heavenly; I was in total balance with myself. That's important if your sign is Libra: You have to achieve that balance, otherwise everything will fall apart.

I basically spent all my time with my new wife. There was so much joy and love in our home that you could enjoy it just by taking a deep breath. When Sebastian's school started in the autumn, they took him to his biological mother. Anastasia had moved to a small town called Bath in western England.

Angela and I lived pretty much isolated from the rest of the world. Every now and then a friend would pop up for dinner or to hang out, so we wouldn't get bored. We also did some spontaneous stuff and often spent time in Palm Springs. It's almost like an oasis in the middle of the desert. Usually me and Angela went there alone, but sometimes Erin, the daughter of

Don Everly (the creative half of the Everly Brothers) and Axl Rose's wife, came along. They're now divorced. Sometimes Angela's friend Dina Russo, who's a bit ding-dong in the head but a loyal friend, tagged along with her fiancé, Patrick Stone, the younger brother of Sharon Stone. On rare occasions, Sharon came too.

Patrick Stone was the best company you could think of to smoke some weed with, but unfortunately he was sometimes a bit slow in the head. I eventually came to the conclusion that he was after some kind of heavy-duty burn-out-your-brain-systematically kind of thing. Patrick loved acid, LSD, but he never said no to crack or freebase or whatever was on offer either. He welcomed everything. The older brother of Sharon and Patrick, Mike Stone, did a long sentence for a massive cannabis crime. Small wonder: No jury member would acquit a person who gets caught with two hundred kilos of high-quality cannabis in his basement.

Mike Stone was a weird guy. He would appear in our lives as if from thin air, hang out for a couple of

Angela and Zeb,
Pomona Fair,
circa '89.

THE GIFT OF LIFE • It's crazy. Life is really a gift from some higher power, a power that's beyond our comprehension. You can see it in the way you come into contact with certain people and how karma works. I've often seen it with my own eyes, because I've been around the world so many times and had the chance to see places that normal people rarely get to see. I've experienced many cultures and learned from them. I've also learned how to be a better person. After you've been an addict and gotten clean, when you look back, it's like seeing a movie of yourself. When you think about the times you were on dope, you wonder how you could've been so dumb. You can only lose with the stuff you use. These powders are not good medicine, not good medicine at all.

days, and then disappear as mysteriously as he had emerged.

In Palm Springs we basked in the sun in an ovenlike heat and refreshed ourselves with margaritas. Angela would obviously drink her favorite drink at the time, piña coladas. Every once in a while I would see from the pool bar—which had become my headquarters—how Angela's bronze-tanned, Italian ass glided past me and splashed into the pool. And Erin would follow, as always, a little behind, a bit exhausted in body and spirit. She was like a student following her Oriental guru.

Sometimes they held each other's hand like two little girls, but mostly they just lazily floated in the pool, Valium-mellow. They were surely a sight for all those happily married and faithful—how faithful, one might ask—husbands to feast their eyes on, these family men taking a quick break from the daily grind of cutthroat American life. I bet at least a couple of those guys were living their fantasies full tilt when they saw the girls in their nonexistent bikinis.

I remember one wonderful, sunny afternoon when all was peaceful and quiet. As if from nowhere, I heard this really disturbing sound, like somebody was screaming their lungs out: "AAARGH! AAARGH!" What the fuck, I thought, had somebody spiked the weed I smoked in the morning? And again,

"GYAAAH!" I realized it was a song I'd written years earlier on a subway train in Stockholm: a Hanoi Rocks classic called "Taxi Driver." I'd written it on my way to rehearsal. Although I didn't have a penny in my pocket, I already had a set goal in life.

Of course I got a bit curious about who was playing the song. I turned my head and saw this tattooed, pierced bartender dancing and singing along to the song: "Yeah, I'll be a milkman for you, baby, I'll milk you any time you want to." I was totally blown away. I mean, what the hell? This guy is juggling three, like, pineapples, and dancing and singing along to "Taxi Driver" in the middle of the desert. I figured I should walk up to him and investigate. I mean, I thought I had left my job far behind, the thing I considered as my job, but then I realized I had totally underestimated the power of mass media. Had I become so big that I was known all around the USA? Well, maybe, but in a way, all of my hard work was finally beginning to pay off. This was what I had always wanted. The more people who hear my tunes, the better. And I never thought I was running away from myself—I had just come to Palm Springs with Angela to get away from the lawyers, managers, and the whole business for a couple of days. But of course I couldn't fight my curiosity, so I walked to the bar, feeling pretty baffled about the whole affair.

"Could I have one more margarita, please?" I asked.

"Sure," he said. "I could have also brought it to you. You don't have to get your drinks yourself."

"Thanks, but I felt like listening to some music."

"Do you like this stuff? This is the best band ever, Hanoi Rocks!"

"Yeah, yeah."

"Oh, you know the band? Great. So you know about music?"

"Yeah, I know that song. I wrote it. And this solo you hear, it's me playing guitar."

There was complete silence for a couple of seconds. I watched his face light up with utter disbelief and surprise. Anybody could have seen it. And then his facial expression changed, almost as in slow motion:

"Oh fuck, you look just like—"

"Yeah, I am Andy McCoy," I said quietly.

"Wow, I should've recognized you instantly. You look just like in the videos and pictures, except for that Zorro moustache. Goddamn, this is an honor! What do you want to drink? Hey, from now on, your money's no good here. All drinks are on the house—and those two beauties"—pointing at Angela and Erin—"they're yours too, right?"

— SHERIFF —

"Yeah, okay, if the drinks are free for the girls too, I guess I could have a drink with them," I said.

"Hey, come here," I yelled to Angela. Erin needed no invitation—she followed Angela like a little dog. I introduced them to the bartender: "Honey, please meet..."

I had to ask the bartender's name.

"Greg."

"Hey Angela, meet my new friend Greg."

"Nice to meet you," the girls said unpretentiously.

Well, in the end, this free drink policy must've cost the bar about $2,500. But you know, he wanted to buy us a drink. While the three of us were partying, I got word from the hotel reception that one mightily incensed Mr. Axl Rose had tried to find his lost fiancée. I'd had no idea that the two were fighting again when we left Los Angeles.

IT WAS NICE TO HAVE A BREAK IN PALM SPRINGS and hang out in the sun, have a massage, swim, and go shopping. I found this horribly overpriced shop that sold Indian stuff, and of course I turned out to be a gold mine for them. I bought all kinds of ghost catchers, mandalas, turquoise and silver bracelets—well, basically everything. Too much money, too little common sense.

One day I walked out of that Indian store carrying a statue as big as me. It was an Indian chief, very elaborate handicraft, carved out of a single piece of redwood. A beautiful work of art. When Angela saw it, she totally lost it: "How the hell are we gonna get that back to Los Angeles?" I guess she had a point, because we had driven there in her BMW. Angela had an eighteen-cylinder deluxe sport model BMW—maybe not the best car for moving your stuff, but very handy for getting from one place to another fast.

Then I got an idea: Maybe I could shove it in through the sunroof. The only problem was that the statue's head and shoulders didn't fit. When we drove back to Los Angeles, that Indian statue proudly stuck out of the sunroof, feathers and all. It was like a reminder to all the cars that passed us:

"Maybe I look like some kind of navigator now, but this land will always remain ours, although you stole it from us. You who made us bleed and die, I remind you of the fact that this is Indian land!"

We drove through the desert, old Indian land. Erin sat in the backseat with "the Chief," my new friend, and I was rolling joints in the front seat. Angela was driving, and Black Uhuru was blasting out on the car stereo at maximum volume. This was just one of the many trips to that place where old people go to die and rich people to have fun.

THAT BARTENDER, GREG, the fan with the tattoos and body piercings, later became my friend, and we've been friends ever since. Greg drove Angela and me around Palm Springs in this really cool, gaudy, red and white '59 Cadillac, maybe the most beautiful Caddy I've ever seen. A rock 'n' roll car if ever there was one. It was the coolest model Cadillac ever produced, with the largest possible—what are they called in Finnish?—wings on the back. Fins.

Angela and I went to have dinner at Greg's house and met his lovely wife and baby. We had a fun night and took it real easy. Greg told us that he came from a pretty rich family, and that he wanted to have a couple of years off before he took over his dad's company. About two years later he called me from Colorado. He had twenty-three employees working for him, and he said we could visit him anytime we wanted. Of course, we meet whenever we're around there and have some time.

In Los Angeles we returned to our normal, chilled-out life. George Nicks had become my new personal assistant. He shuttled my guitars around town, got me booze and cigarettes, and ran whatever errands I needed. At that time, Angela was devoting all her energy to studying. Sometimes we'd throw a party, a normal L.A.-star type of shindig, or I'd venture out on my own hunting trips, combing pawn shops for curios and old guitars. Sometimes we went down to Del Mar to visit the legendary Eddie Nahan, known in New York as "Eddie the Hat." Eddie owned the best antique shop on the Southwest Coast, just a couple of minutes from the Mexican border. It was called the Ivory Horse, and shit, I spent so much money there it's insane. I love Eddie and his New York, whiplash, Jewish sense of humor, especially when he's a bit drunk.

Del Mar was a place Angela and I went to chill out. I adored it, and so did my wife. Looking back, I think Del Mar really enriched my life. In my memories, it is the most chilled-out place in the world. My son now lives and goes to school there, enjoying a normal childhood with his grandparents and cousin. I noticed early on that my kind of nomadic lifestyle just doesn't suit a child.

Back to Los Angeles. I learned that Steven Adler, who was still the drummer in Guns N' Roses at the time, lived just fifty yards away from me. By then, we had already lived at Laurel Terrace for four months or so. The fact that Steve was our neighbor was not good news. There were a lot of rumors about him circulating in L.A., and one of the heaviest was that he had a serious relationship with the most seducing and destructive gal of 'em all—a golden girl called heroin.

I really knew I had to stay away, but as I was taking a walk one day, there he stood. It was too late to turn and pretend I hadn't seen him.

"Hi, Andy, what are you doing here? What, are you living in that giant fuckin' castle? Wow! Cool. What are you doing tonight? You should come over later."

I went and we got high. Some first-class Mexican heroin and cocaine, totally pure. I realized I didn't even want to, but I just followed him. Steven's house was okay, not as big as ours. He led me to a darkened bedroom, where pitch-black, triple velvet curtains hung over the window. The vibe was lead-heavy, almost like I had stepped into a time machine and traveled back

LEGENDS • For me, Iggy Pop is a legend, Mike Monroe is a legend, and I'm a legend too, but I guess there are no other legends in Finland at the moment. Remu is a legend, yeah, and Dave is almost there. He should write another song like "I'm Gonna Roll," and then he'd become a legend in my book, too. But as a person, I think he's great—for starters, he calls beer "blues oil."

a century. It was a true opium den.

Well, I went over for about four days, supposedly to jam with him. I walked over to Steven's house with my '54 Les Paul Junior in hand, pretending that we were gonna jam, though in reality we just did Mexican horse and nodded. It didn't take long for Angela to find out what was going down, maybe a day or two at the most. I remember the day when Steven had given me some dope the previous night so I could have a morning fix. That's when I realized I was plunging head over heels into addiction again. I fixed myself for the last time as Angela was sleeping next to me, looking ever so sweet and serene. But when she woke up, she was all over the place within seconds:

"You fuckin' cocksucker motherfucker! You just can't stay away from that shit, can you?!" I realized Angela was looking me straight in the eye, and that my pupils were obviously pretty nonexistent.

"It's that motherfucker Steven, isn't it?" she asked.

"I know it's that goddamn, unfortunate ass-licker! That bitch does anything to have some company!"

Then Angela went to inflict some total psychological torture on Steven. You know, an Italian girl who's fuckin' mad and basically wants your balls is someone you just don't mess with. Believe me, I know. I just hoped she didn't carry that small Derringer handgun I had given to her. Or maybe it would've been for the best—with the gun, at least it would have been all over sooner.

After that episode, Steven vanished from the picture and everything returned to normal. I had only been using for four days. I didn't get hooked again, thank God, and thank Angela.

A routine was building in our daily lives. We often had dinner with my lawyer David Codikow, the only person I know whose imagination is as sick as mine. David negotiated my Polygram deal. Caz, who had been my publisher through three different companies since I was seventeen, had become the president of publishing, so I got a great publishing deal from BMG-Virgin USA. In the evenings, Angela and me made sweet love. Angela's tan body was like a statue of Venus herself. I've always known that the best things in life are free: music, good friends, and the kind of love that's shared and as intense and passionate as ours was, and still is. It's more than free—it's almost like a blessing. That kind of love has a life of its own, and if you tend to it like we've done, through good times and bad times, it will grow really strong and powerful.

ONE FINE DAY AT LAUREL TERRACE, Erin showed up. I was watching TV and half-listening as she cried hysterically to Angela. She was begging for pills, sobbing that it was time to end it all. "Shut up already," Angela said. Erin explained that while driving drunk, she'd tried to crash her car off Mulholland Drive at a spot where there's a 150-yard drop down the cliff. It's a perfect spot if you want to commit vehicular suicide—there's not much left of you after a 150-yard drop. That's where James Dean and a lot of other people were killed. But Erin didn't have the guts—she was just vying for attention.

She begged me for Valium that my doctor had prescribed me, just like, "Andy, give me a couple…"

Angela tried listening. Erin always had the same story: "Axl tried to kill me! He even ripped off my nipple ring!"

Granted, it sounded horrible, and I started thinking that maybe it wasn't all bullshit—although I knew that some of the stuff she accused Axl of was blown out of proportion. Angela later told me she thought Erin was disturbed enough to rip off the ring herself, just so she could blame Axl and get attention. Erin was a poor little rich kid, like Veronica Sellers, another similar figure in our circle of friends. She's the daughter of Britt Ekland and Peter Sellers. Lou Adler is her stepfather, the guy who produced *The Rocky Horror Picture Show*, some Carole King and Mamas & the Papas stuff, Cheech & Chong flicks, the Who's rock opera *Tommy*, and also discovered Otis Redding. Lou had become a pretty close friend. But yeah, Erin would do anything to get some attention. Angela was right.

Eventually Angela became really worried. She realized that maybe Erin was already beyond help. Erin just got into self-destruction mode so fast, and sometimes Angela just sighed and gave her the pills when she begged.

Erin was around all the time. She actually sort of came between me and Angela. The neighbors found it weird. It looked like I had two women, but even the thought of touching her disgusted me.

Later on that same day Erin threatened to kill herself. Angela entered the room while I was watching a movie. "Where the fuck is Erin?" she asked. "I left her sleeping in our bed."

I went to check out the upstairs bedroom, and sure enough, Erin had disappeared. Angela thought for a minute and remembered that Erin had wanted to visit Steven next door. Erin had already asked me for heroin, but I had told her she wouldn't find that stuff in my house no more. Erin even offered to give us five hundred bucks if we copped a fix together. If I had been a junkie, I'd have instantly made a $480 profit. But no way! You never introduce no one to heroin—that's a matter of principle.

At the time, Steven was just about to get sacked from Guns N' Roses. Angela and me looked at each other and said simultaneously: "Steven's!" Erin was surely at Steven's. Suddenly all that talk about suicide took on a whole new meaning, and we realized it was a young woman's cry for help—a woman who didn't want to live anymore. Angela instantly said to me: "Andy, you run to Steven's house right now! Where else could she be? Her Jeep's still parked in front of our house. Go see if there's evil afoot!"

I could tell from Angela's face that she was really worried. She told me to call as soon as I could. I ran over like some motherfucking rapist with the cops after me, fuck, and a pack of bloodhounds, too. I rang the bell for at least three minutes, until Steven Adler came to the door. He looked like an Alphabet City junkie, not stylish at all, the motherfucker, scratching his armpits, shit, even his balls—really fuckin' disgusting.

He tried to open the door and finally managed to get the safety chain off. I rushed in, like, "Erin, where is she? Is she okay?" "Oh, she's in the bedroom," Steven mumbled. "She's turning blue." He said it so calmly as if nothing in the world mattered a bit. I became really pissed off and yelled at him: "Steven, how much did you give her?"

Well, at least I had a good idea what she had taken. No answer from Steven. I grabbed him by the shirt and slammed him against the wall. I asked again: "Steven, this could be a matter of life and death! How much?!"

I panicked. I tried to revive Erin. I slapped her face. I gave her mouth to mouth. I kept banging on her chest. Then I remembered what my late friend, my wife's cousin, Johnny Thunders taught me: If you see somebody overdosing, you must use buprenorphine, or even just salt. Buprenorphine is ten times more effective. It stops the division of heroin in the body, and salt does the same thing to an extent. I finally found a vein and did what Johnny taught me.

I screamed at Steven to call a fuckin' ambulance. It was useless. That fuckin' chickenshit was so scared that he couldn't do anything. He was just like, "No, man, I gotta hide, fuck, I'll go to the shower."

Well, no wonder the guy broke a sweat: He had just given our good, mutual friend her first fix of smack, and she was about to die in his house. But I still couldn't understand how somebody could say something like that, without any sympathy for human life. It made me sick, but I kept on banging Erin's chest and everything. Finally she began to breathe, very slowly and faintly, and I could feel a feeble pulse. Then I called Angela: "You call the ambulance now. I can't do that, I have my hands full trying to save her life."

I scattered ice on Erin's half-dead body and tried forcing

some strong coffee into her mouth. I tried to walk her around, simultaneously slapping her face. Every once in a while I had to lay her on the floor so I could bang her heart and administer mouth-to-mouth resuscitation.

"Erin, Erin, you're a strong woman! Breathe!"

I prayed to the holy and good Saint Sara-la-Kali, the patron angel of us Gypsies.

Angela came over with

JAMLO SARISALMI

Judie Aronson, her actress friend who lived next door. Judie was always around, although she wasn't a part of the rock 'n' roll scene. Now she surely realized what kind of people her neighbors were. She and Angela both went white in the face. Angela came to help and took care of first aid, I mean resuscitation, while I kept banging Erin's heart. I didn't give a fuck if her rib bones cracked, as long as her heart kept beating.

I took a five-second breather. It seemed like, shit, Erin's panties were down to her ankles. Remember this: Erin never did drugs, she sometimes took a Valium and sometimes had a drink, but never simultaneously. Although you couldn't deny that her downward spiral had already begun. In many respects she was like a child, a very naive person who always needed somebody around. I think Axl had written their huge hit "Sweet Child O'

Mine" about her for that reason: Erin was like a small child. When I saw her there with her pants down and almost dying, I couldn't help wondering if Steven had done something to her while she was out cold. What a cocksucker if so!

We could just about feel Erin's pulse when we heard the ambulance and the LAPD arrive outside the house. The ambulance guys got to work right away, and I mean instantly. Goddammit, I so respect these guys; they dedicate their lives to helping others. That's something we should all learn, even if it's just small things, because then this world would be so much better to live in.

I watched them take care of Erin, and she looked almost like a doll. When they asked me what she had taken, I had to tell the truth: "Heroin, I don't how much, maybe also Valium. I don't know about the amounts."

I talked to the cops. Steve was still hiding in the shower. Motherfuckin' fuck, what a chickenshit! Me, Angela, and Judie, Angela's actress friend, began to fear the worst. Would Erin pull through?

"We don't know," the paramedics said. They tried to kick-start her heart.

First time: "DUM!"

"Pump it, the pulse is rising, the pulse is rising, yeah, we got her. Hey, she's breathing again!"

They carried Erin out, and the ambulance chief asked me: "Have you taken a first-aid course or something? I'm sure you have."

"No, man, you're talking to the wrong guy," I said.

He took me by the arm: "You've just saved a life. Without you, we would have carried her out in a different kind of bag altogether. In a black one, if you know what I mean."

"You mean she would've died?" I asked.

"Yes," he said.

A couple of cops came to shake my hand.

"Thanks, man, you saved her life."

I watched as the cops and ambulances left and took Erin away. I was starting to feel bad. For the first time in my life—although I had already kicked the habit myself—I was struck that heroin is really public enemy number one. It's first-rate poison. It's not just a "small personal problem," you know what I mean, like, "I just have a small cold." That's what I used to say before the withdrawal symptoms got so bad that I couldn't even get out of bed. The craziest thing is I never received any thanks from Erin, although she reappeared in our life later on and naturally messed everything up once again.

Later that night Axl Rose called me and said, "Thanks, Andy, how can I ever thank you? I really owe you big-time. Whatever you need—money, whatever—you only have to call." Truth be told, he still owes me, and I hope he still remembers that, because one day I might really need him to return the favor. I take these things real seriously. He and Erin are now divorced—thank God, because that relationship was just so sick and violent.

Later that same evening it all came out in tears, and I cried together with Angela. The number one thing was a deep psychological hatred of drugs, and then I thought about the fact that I had been called some kind of hero. Of course it made me feel good. I mean, I've been called every name in the book, and "hero" was a far cry from the other titles. So it felt really good. I still don't know to this day whether I prevented Erin's great jump into eternity, or if maybe she was angry at me because of that. But when she reads this one day, I hope she remembers all the good times she must have had since then. Also with me and Angela. Without this one McCoy, all that would've been thrown in the trash. Life, the greatest gift of 'em all, would've just been tossed into a grave. She wanted to screw it all up. But it was great that she could still be forgiven.

After that incident, I knew Steven's days in Guns N' Roses were numbered. It really didn't take a clairvoyant to see he had been given far too many breaks, and enough was enough. A couple days later, I saw three extra long limousines pull up to Steven's house. Alan—that is, Alan Niven, the manager of Guns N' Roses—stepped out of the car with Axl. Then about five guys who looked like lawyers marched in. I wondered what was going on. I bet Steven, stoned as shit, sputtered something like: "What do I get this time? Are you gonna give me money? Where do I sign?"

You signed your life away, that's what you did. I wonder if it was worth the money they gave you. Of course I've learned myself that what you do to others will happen to you. That's the karmic law.

A couple months later Steven sued Guns N' Roses, claiming that they had turned him into a junkie. Slash and Izzy Stradlin had allegedly encouraged him to shoot smack. He

95

blamed especially Slash. Well, Slash has the biggest heart, or one of the biggest hearts, in that band, and unfortunately it was me who introduced him to that scene. But the most surprising thing was that Steven won the case: He got a million bucks, tax-free, and blew it all on heroin. So that was Steven's story with the biggest rock band in the world. He really screwed up that one.

Let that be a lesson for you what a mix of heroin and cocaine can do, especially if they're perfectly blended and taken intravenously. The last I heard of Steven, he got chased down by LAPD helicopters. He had passed out in his car, nodding out on smack, and somebody had called the cops about a half-conscious driver. Jail, that's where you ended up, Steven. Maybe you learned something there.

Oh, I forgot, Steven: If you're currently doing time, watch out when you bend over to pick up the soap.

Love, Andy.

I FIRST MET ANGELA WHEN I WAS HAVING DINNER at some Mexican restaurant in downtown Hollywood. Izzy Stradlin, the guitarist of Guns N' Roses, appeared at my table, followed by Angela. They were celebrating the birthday of club promoter Mike Canters, and I guess all of Guns N' Roses was there. I started talking to Angela. At the time, I was in the process of separating from Anastasia. We chatted for a while, nothing more, but I think we both felt a connection. Every time we met after that, we always hung out together.

Maybe it was love at first sight or something equally instantaneous. The second time I met Angela was at the Roxy, but she was so out of it that I just wanted to run away. I bought her a drink and told some guy to take it to her and tell her I had to leave. Next day Angela told me she felt really bad about the way she had behaved. But hey, we were still young, and to party hearty was the order of the day.

I think it finally clicked one night when Transvision Vamp played the Roxy. Angela worked there, and we had booked a balcony where we could watch the band without being disturbed. Right there we touched each other for the first time and all. There was also a funny incident when a guy called Cheeseboy was so zonked out on pills that he tried to attack me. About then, me and Anastasia were about to split up and fought like fuck. Cheeseboy told me that Stacy had broken all the windows in his house. I told him that it was no fault of mine, that he should ask Stacy for the money, since she was the one who broke his goddamn windows. Somehow Angela managed to get rid of that guy.

Then Izzy invited me to see GNR open up for the Stones. I went with a friend called Eddie, and it was really boring, actually. It was a typical arena gig: too many people, and unless you were at the side of the stage, you could see nothing. Well, I watched most of the Guns N' Roses set and went backstage to say hi to Slash. Slash said he had some weed, so we decided to roll a joint, but because we had no papers, I said I'd go ask the Stones if they had some. Ronnie Wood would surely have some Rizlas, I thought. I started walking towards the Stones' dressing room, and I ran across Angela. And that's when it happened. I never went back to Slash; instead, Angela and I left together.

I still remember Angela wearing jeans and a black derby hat that night. She had rented a limo for the evening and said we had to talk. I, too, felt it was about time we talked. Angela told me all about her feelings, and I told her all about mine, and for the first time in my life, it felt like I was really, truly in love.

Everything happened pretty fast after that. It took about a week for us to move in together. I just couldn't stand Stacy's constant drug use anymore. When I returned from the Iggy Pop tour, I was totally clean, but then I came home to a woman who was high as a kite all the time. It would've been just a matter of time before I'd relapse. If you're a former junkie and you have to watch somebody else do dope, you'll soon do it yourself. It

was time for me to leave Stacy and kick heroin. I had found the love of my life.

Andy and Angela, Justice of the Peace, Los Angeles, USA: The marriage is official.

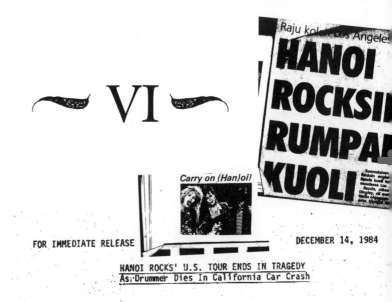

~ VI ~

Carry on (Han)oi!

FOR IMMEDIATE RELEASE   DECEMBER 14, 1984

HANOI ROCKS' U.S. TOUR ENDS IN TRAGEDY
As Drummer Dies In California Car Crash

Let's move on. There's not been much talk about the last days of Hanoi Rocks, about the general vibe and so on. I remember that we had just completed a very successful tour in Japan. Everything worked like a charm. Money was coming in by the wagonload. We spent four days off in London, just taking it easy. We went shopping for some clothes. We had the money, we had everything any of us had ever wanted. We flew to the States in really high spirits, thinking now we were gonna show the Yanks. We had already done the groundwork and toured there many times. Los Angeles was probably the only US city we still hadn't played, and our two nights in L.A. sold out in less than twenty minutes. Ironically, Angela, my future wife, was promoting those shows with John Harrington.

VINCE NEIL BUSTED FOR MANSLAUGHTER: It's a tale. One that certainly could have been

Singer charged as crasn kill:

Redondo Beach, Calif. (Combined Dispatches)—The lead singer of the rock band Mötley Crüe faced manslaughter and drunk driving charges yesterday after he

Punk drummer killed

REDONDO BEACH, Calif. (UPI)

Wharton, 23, and Dingley were ... in 1972 Pantera when

TOMS RIVER, NJ
OBSERVER
D. 23,172 S. 22,653

We hit the road and everybody started partying like crazy right off the bat. First up was New York. Susan Blond, who was part of the high society, introduced us to Andy Warhol and the so-called artist elite of New York. I was totally fuckin' disinterested. Warhol seemed to be the eavesdropper type; he rarely talked at all. I thought Mike would get his undivided attention, but I guess I pulled the shortest straw, because he was all over my ass. He gave me a couple paintings that are currently at Angela's parents' place. I hear they're worth a bazillion dollars these days.

That was the first time I had the chance to snort all the coke I wanted. Everybody wondered, "What the fuck's the matter with that guy? He's running to the toilet every three minutes." It was as if I was only interested in...well, another line of nose candy. Oh man, it was a crazy time. The barmy stuff you pull when you're young. There's no way I'd ever do something like that anymore. You get some sense into your head with age. Anyway, the tour went on, and each gig was fuckin' awesome.

Then, in one of the smaller towns on the East Coast, Mike Monroe sprained his ankle. Of course it was originally my fault. I broke a bottle onstage, and when Mike jumped off a side-fill stage monitor, he landed on a big shard of glass. Fortunately it was not very sharp, but he twisted his ankle. We had to cancel some gigs, but we still drove onward to Atlanta.

Tour buses in the U.S. are really built for touring. Nowadays each bunk bed is 4.9 feet wide and seven feet long, and they all have lockable curtains. They're great for chilling out, because each bunk has a mini-TV, a VCR, and a stereo system. The bus had clean sheets, showers, toilets, big stereos in both the front and the back lounges, plus a TV and VCR. There we partied and fucked. I played a lot of guitar in the back lounge. It got pretty insane.

Seppo had to have a word with Razzle, because he drank like fuck and snorted, swallowed, or shot everything that was on offer. Even I started to think that this guy wouldn't live for long, but of course I had no idea what would happen. I had cleaned up my act and kicked heroin, because I was determined s in accident

Helsingin konsertit pidetään
Sam jättää
Hanoi Rock

s arrested on suspi-
-iving and vehicular

was to perform at Hollyw
Palace nightclub next weekend.
"We haven't discussed that ye

that Hanoi would finally break big. After hearing about the Los Angeles Palace gigs selling out in less than half an hour, we really looked forward to playing L.A. We were just about to step up to the arenas, first as a support act. The top tier is to be an arena band all over the world. And it had all started with a small boy's dream.

We arrived in Los Angeles. The Mötley Crüe guys heard we were in town, so of course Tommy Lee and Nikki Sixx came to say hi. Tommy Lee is the only guy in that band whom I can still call a friend.

Tommy came first, and we had a blast: We drank, smoked shit, and partied like only young guys can. There were no girls around, it was that exclusive. We wanted to be just among gentlemen. While waiting for the gig, me and Mike were supposed to do press for a couple of days.

Vince, whose real name is Vincent Neil Wharton, or maybe Wart-on, shit, on that night he decided to drink and drive. And this is a lesson for you all: Never drink and drive. It's not even about how much you have drunk—you should never drive after drinking alcohol. Of course Vince had to show off his new car, because Mötley Crüe were reaping the first fruits of their success. At that moment, Hanoi was enjoying much wider recognition. Nikki Sixx kept on saying: "You're the great white hope, you're the great white hope!" He just wouldn't shut up, so I had to say: "Shut up, we're Hanoi Rocks, that's what we are!"

102

And suddenly they disappeared, Razzle and Vince. Vince had a wife who was seven months pregnant, and she was the first to get worried. I was so drunk that I didn't realize anything for a while. Sami had passed out on the couch—he was such a lightweight when he was younger. Mike was in his hotel room. At least he wanted to take care of his body and mind then, as I hope he still does. So he had gone to bed, because we had a pretty long and tiring trip behind us.

We couldn't find Razzle and Vince anywhere, so we finally decided that Tommy should drive. He hadn't drunk that much, maybe three or four beers, so he would have only gotten a fine and maybe lost his driver's license for a couple of months for DUI. Besides, American beer is so weak that Tommy was acting completely sober. I had drunk more, hard liquor.

As we were driving, we passed some fuckin' accident. Tommy looked around. I was like, "Didn't you say that he had a red car?" There had been a red car by the side of the road. "Fuck, man," Tommy said. He turned the car around. We arrived at the scene and I instantly saw Razzle's Stetson hat, this suede Stetson with the Hanoi red rose logo on the front. I asked what the hell had happened. The cop told me that all he knew was that the other guy had been taken to the hospital. I watched as they pushed the handcuffed Vince into a cop car. He was able to walk by himself. There was no blood anywhere.

ROCK 'N' ROMANIS • Rock 'n' rollers are pretty much the Gypsies of this century. I have it in my blood, and I'm glad some whiteys live like our ancestors, making a living traveling from town to town, playing music and entertaining people. The road that has brought me here is the same road that will take me away. This is the road of a Gypsy, me. And when I walk along this road, I write new songs about my experiences, the things I've seen and everything that's affected or touched me in some way. I'm happy to have been born in Finland, in the place where I was born, and now I'm here where I am. Many people never travel a road as long as mine. I know that for a fact.

At Seppo's place. Andy, Sami, and Moses from the Apocalypse of St. John.

Shit, if I had been a cop, I would've beat the living shit out of him. Drunk drivers kill children and innocent people.

Anyway, the cops told us the name of the hospital. I asked if I could take the hat, because it belonged to my friend. "No, because there might be a criminal case," he said. I pointed it out to them, and they said I could pick it up later from the precinct, but when I went there later, they had never heard of the fuckin' hat. Fuckin' cops stole it for themselves.

We parked the car, ran inside the hospital, and asked people at the reception desk where the ambulances arrive—like, where's the intensive care, where did they bring him? We told 'em there had just been an accident at Redondo Beach. They directed us down a hallway, and pretty soon a doctor came out to ask us: "Does either one of you know this guy called Razzle? Is either one of you a relative?"

I told him I was not a relative but I was almost like family. "I regret to inform you that your friend is dead," the doctor said. "He left this world at so-and-so hours. I can only assure you that he didn't feel any pain."

My whole world shattered. Everything I had built up since I was a small kid came crashing down! We had a perfect band, everything was within our grasp, and then it all crumbled. I was in a really chaotic state of mind, but I knew I had to stay strong. I called Seppo Vesterinen, who accompanied us on the tour, and told him he should come to the hospital and bring the whole band. He asked me what had happened, and I...I mean, what can you say in a situation like that? I've never learned how to break that kind of news, anyway. I just told them to get there and promised to explain the whole thing when they arrived. I just beat around the bush, like, "No, it's nothing, I just need to sort something out."

The guys came to the hospital. Sami was crying hysterically: "Where is Razzle?" I guess he had woken up from his stupor and heard that we had gone looking for Razzle. Nasse just sat there, legs spread wide, hands between his legs. Nobody said or heard anything. You could just see the tears trickling down.

I told 'em I would kill Vince. Tommy Lee was crying and cursed the guy, and said he'd beat the shit out of him. But no kind of money could bring Razzle back. That's why we decided not to sue Mötley Crüe. It would have seemed like we put a price on his head. They paid a couple of millions to Raz's parents, but

I think the money went to the wrong address, because his father got it. Razzle's dad had kicked him out when he was sixteen, and the next time he saw his son was in a casket. Raz met his mother secretly because his father didn't approve.

I tried to remain strong. Mike Monroe totally lost it. We took a limo back to the hotel, and after that all hell broke loose. Goddammit, there were people from the *New York Times*, CBS News, Satellite USA, any kind of media you could imagine, from *Rolling Stone* to basically fuckin' Estonian TV. I accepted no calls. In my room, I still managed to keep my cool and called Anna. She was crying. It seemed like the whole world already knew about it. It showed how big the band had become. Or how small the world seemed now.

Fuck, man, then I found Razzle's diaries. I still have them in my possession. They're private, and I guess the only people I'll allow to read them are the former band members. They contain a lot of memories, because Razzle wrote down everything, all the crazy parties.

Somehow I managed not to cry. I hadn't lost it yet. Then I heard the George Michael song "Careless Whisper" for the first time. The radio DJ said it was the world premiere. The chorus went: "I'm never gonna dance again, guilty feet have got no rhythm." It hit home, straight through my armor, and I fuckin' cried and cried. Once again one of the good ones had died. But I'll still meet him in the next world. I am so fuckin' stubborn because I'm also doing this for Razzle. I'm still flying the flag.

We decided that the rest of the band would fly to London, and me and Mike would stay in L.A. for a few weeks. I

Ruisrock '83.

Pre-Ruisrock, Hanoi Rocks and Jimi Sumén.

went to see Razzle's body after they prepared it for the funeral, and it almost felt like it was one of his jokes again. I had the feeling he would jump up any second and laugh: "Ha-ha, fuck, I really had you this time, didn't I?" He looked so alive, lying there in his favorite white suit, frilled shirt, and all his favorite jewelry. Mike walked out and I stayed to kiss Razzle goodbye and say a prayer to holy Saint Sara-la-Kali. Raz was ciao. But we'd meet again.

HANOI DIDN'T BREAK UP only because of Razzle's death. There was also the thing that I had met Anastasia—Stacy—Mike

Man, her breath stinks! Sami and Anna after
the last Finnish gig, at Kulttuuritalo.

Monroe's girlfriend and Stiv Bators' wife. The situation was made more difficult by the fact that Sami was fucking my girlfriend Anna, and apparently Anna was pregnant. Sami had already said before Razzle's death that he would leave the band after the tour. So basically we hadn't lost one but two members. I also believe Stacy was the reason why me and Mike lost each other for much too long. It was hard, and the band's personal chemistry was incredibly tricky. We'd just been too close for too long. And it didn't help that instantly after losing two members, we were sent on tour to make more money.

For the first time in my life, I told Mike and Nasse that I would just fuck off. I'd go to L.A. to shoot dope. I thought, what the fuck would it matter if I did or didn't? I didn't care if I lived or died.

I sent out for some heroin, and I developed a habit almost instantly. A girl called Susan was staying at my place in London. I'll never know who Susan really was, she was just this really beautiful Scottish girl with blond, curly hair. She had no place to stay, and she was also good company because she had the same problem I did. There was no sex; I just had money and a big bag of heroin at home, over a hundred grams. I let her crash there and jack up. One day she bought a boat ticket to Argentina. The trip was to last over a month. She said if that didn't clean her up, nothing would. I later found out she had succeeded in staying clean. Good luck, wherever you are, and greetings.

I decided to go to Sri Lanka, because I needed a vacation and wanted to kick my habit. The first week I drank like a fish. Each night I'd fall into this half-conscious stupor that lasted for one or two hours, but before long it got a bit easier. Some bush doctor gave me a batch of "medicine" and told me to take three pills a day. Well, I tried a quarter of a pill, and I was so fuckin' out of it that I just kept ordering ice cream until the cows came home. I had about thirteen servings before I dragged myself to my suite, where I finally collapsed after staying up for practically a week. I slept for a couple of days.

I spent the rest of the vacation writing new songs, walking on the beach, and buying these really cool antique wood statues that were later so insolently destroyed by British customs at Gatwick airport. "What's inside of these?" they sneered. Fuck, they knew there was nothing because they had X-rayed them! I had to kiss goodbye my estimated 2 to 5 thousand percent profits, but fortunately they didn't spot the gemstones. I had bought some cheap imitation jewelry in London and exchanged the rhinestones for emeralds and rubies Sri Lanka and put them back on. Shit, I looked like a jewelry store mannequin, but I got the gems through the customs, including two big rocks that earned me a handsome transport fee. So thank you so much, customs assholes: You don't see what's in front of you, but you ruin these two hundred-year-old antique statues because you thought you'd find some—what? Nothing, for fuck's sake!

My health came back to me in Sri Lanka. I wrote a lot of songs, most of the stuff on Suicide Twins' *Silver Missiles and Nightingales* LP, and I really had a great time. I basically had a whole manor to myself: four or five servants, a swimming pool, and the ocean only a hundred feet away. I was there for seven months. I kicked my habit and returned to London clean and healthy.

110

— SHERIFF —

GUITARS

I think the first guitar I got was an old Fender Telecaster, probably from the early '60s. My dad bought it for me. I had to sell it to get a three-pickup '58 Gibson Les Paul Black Beauty that I still have. It's the same guitar you can see on the covers of Pelle Miljoona's <u>Moottoritie on kuuma</u> and the first Hanoi Rocks album. Guitars have become a big part of my life. I've collected 'em, I've lost some wonderful axes, and I've also found some marvelous ones. The only one I still wish I had snatched was Jimi Hendrix's painted Gibson Flying V. It was on auction, and I would have really loved to get that one. The starting bid was $20,000, and I said, I'm willing to pay $40,000, tops. Well, it went for $50,000. Thinking back, I would've paid that, too. I'm a serious guitar freak.

I guess my current fave is the '53 Les Paul Junior Single Cutaway. I also have two of these cool '58 Black Beauties and one '62, but the one I got as a kid is still my favorite. I also have a '64 Firebird with a custom middle pickup and a new tremolo arm—I would've had to wait for six weeks to get a Gibson whammy bar, so I bought an Epiphone. Sometimes I think the whole thing looks like an Epiphone, but the sound instantly tells you it's not. I'm also pretty much in love with a wine-colored '69 Standard that's my favorite Les Paul.

Then I have that Gibson L5S that Albert Järvinen used to play. Once I had to hock that one, too—I got $1,400 for it, and had to buy it back for $3,000. But hey, c'est la vie. Welcome to the world of guitars.

Right now, I use a '46 Regent with a custom '51 or '52 pickup. When you plug it in, the sound is pure magic. I also have a Gibson Limited Edition '58-series Flying V that's really cool. I have numerous Firebirds, Les Pauls, and a really neat, handmade Washburn semiacoustic. It's a Montgomery model; only twenty were made. That's one guitar I will never sell. Then I have some Gibson 135s, 335s—oh yeah, and a cream-colored '62 Les Paul Double Cutaway with three pickups. That's a good axe. There were some others, too, but I think guitar freaks can read more about 'em somewhere else. I did an interview a couple of years ago about my fave guitars.

When it comes to the amps, I still use my 1960s Marshall (it's probably from '68), a Fender Twin, and a Roland 130. Everything's blasted through Marshall 300 cabinets, parallel connection, not series.

Mike, photographer Justin Thomas, and me.

Somewhere in Poland, autumn 1985.

NASSE HAD SHARED AN APARTMENT WITH RAZZLE. He said he couldn't bear to be there alone, so I let him stay at my place while I was in Sri Lanka. When I came back, shit, it was total guitar hell! I mean, I'm a guitar freak myself, I love guitars, but with Nasse's guitars and my guitars there must have been a total of seventy guitars in that apartment. You couldn't walk anywhere without stumbling onto an axe, and I'm talking fine guitars here: '53s, Telecasters, '52s, Les Paul Juniors, fuck, Silvertone Switch Masters, oh man, all these beautiful babies.

I was fuckin' tired when I arrived, and the first thing I saw was a totally wired Nasse. They had done coke and speed and stayed up for five days, or at least four. The mess was unbelievable. I just told them to get the fuck out and I fell asleep.

Then the last sorry episode in the history of Hanoi Rocks began. Who would be chosen for the band? I mean, who had Nasse and Mike chosen for the band while I was in Sri Lanka? They had picked Terry Chimes as the drummer. He had been the original drummer of the Clash and everything. What really surprised me was their choice for bassist: a guy called René Berg, from the Idle Flowers and Soho Vultures. Right off the bat I thought there was something fishy about the guy, but I was like, okay, if you have already rehearsed the songs with him, I guess we can try it out.

We rehearsed for a week in a London studio before it was time to do the last thing we hadn't done. A tour of Poland. And mother of fuck, what a catastrophe that turned out to be. We flew to Germany in a normal plane, a 747, but then we had to change planes, because at the time you couldn't get to Poland in a large plane. We climbed aboard a propeller plane. Seppo, who accompanied us on the tour, totally freaked out. Even on a normal day, he was scared of flying. The doctor gave him a sedative before the flight, and Valium really did the trick along with some vodka and orange juice. Hey, we all have our fears.

Richard Bishop was my manager at the time, and he carried my methadone across the border in a cough syrup bottle, although there was really no need to do that. "Methadone" could've been written in capital letters on the bottle, because we didn't have to go through customs at all. I guess we were some kind of cultural VIPs.

On the first night we went to some restaurants that were probably frequented by the KGB and high-ranking politicians at the time. The food was as good as in any Western restaurant, but man, the people looked so drab. For some reason, René Berg arrived a day later. This was to be his trial by fire. I don't know why, but I was feeling down all the time. Razzle's death was still haunting me. I'm sure it was haunting Mike like hell too.

My former school pal,

then my band pal,

then my junkie pal,

then...

We arrived in Poland, and René couldn't open his suitcase, so he ran to me for help. I managed to force it open, and to my horror, it sprang apart like overpacked suitcases usually do. All kinds of pills fell out: red pills, green pills, yellow pills, black pills, blue pills, pills of all colors and shapes. Give me a fuckin' break, I said to myself, now we've got a pillhead in tow too.

On the second day the word got around that we were in Warsaw, and groupies began gathering at the hotel. René picked up the first whore he saw. Later, sitting next to Nasse in a bar, he bragged to the chick: "This is my guitarist." The guy hadn't even played a single gig with us. I heard Nasse didn't take that very well, and I can understand why not.

It was a routine gig. We just went through the motions. Somehow the feeling was dead. Terry Chimes did his job admirably, but our bass player continued to screw things up. Everything was just so horrible, right down to his stage moves. The following night we told the roadies to only give him a five-foot bass cord so he would have to stand right in front of his amp. We played these packed arena halls and the crowds went nuts, but the band was starting to show fatigue.

The next night we were still wondering what the hell we should do with René. We decided we'd kill the lights over him so he wouldn't be in anybody's way. Terry's playing was great again, and Nasse was falling-down drunk.

On the first night in Warsaw, while checking out the arena I met a couple of young guys. I asked them if it was possible to find some weed over there. "Yeah, yeah," they said. I thought I'd give them twenty bucks, so if they ripped me off, it would only be for twenty bucks. When I came to the hotel five hours later, I heard a voice, but I didn't see anybody.

"Psst, Andy, psst!"

What the fuck! I looked again but saw nobody.

"Psst, Andy…"

I had totally forgotten about those guys. They'd brought this big food bag full of weed for us, prime bud, for just twenty bucks. I wondered if it was a setup, if the next minute the KGB—or whoever took care of things like that in Poland at the time—would come and book me. So I instantly handed over the bag to our manager, Seppo Vesterinen.

We had our work cut out for us, and I tell you it really was a lot of work to get rid of the whole bag of weed. We smoked it everywhere: in hotel lobbies and receptions, nightclubs, and restaurants. "Uh, this is European tobacco, Western cigarettes, you know!" Ha-ha! I guess our photographer Justin Thomas didn't sleep a wink during the whole week; he just partied like crazy and scored chicks after the gigs.

We had our own bus. One time when we stopped to have a pee in the middle of nowhere, we heard somebody playing guitar nearby. It was so dark we couldn't make out where the sound was coming from, but after walking for a while we found a party going on. They were totally amazed to see us, Western guys who looked like we did, and they welcomed us to join the party. There were a couple of guitars lying around, so Mike and me played some blues standards while the local guys brought us food and drinks.

After a while we decided it was time to go. Everybody went to have a pee again, and climbed back on the bus. Before the bus left, we made sure that everybody was inside. After five minutes, Justin Thomas—who had basically been screaming full tilt for a couple of days already, and was beginning to get on everybody's nerves—started crying: "Nasse is missing, Nasse is missing!" We told him to shut the fuck up. Everybody had had enough of his hollering. We fell asleep and woke up in the next town. Where was it again—I think we did six gigs in Poland. Or was it five? Anyway, we realized that, shit, Nasse was nowhere to be seen.

I later found out Nasse had heard our bus leaving, but he'd had his suit pants on, and when he started running, the pants dropped to his ankles and he tripped. He couldn't even run after the bus. Nasse then walked barefoot for a couple of miles along the road. They eventually found him at some bus stop at ten in the morning. He had been too afraid to sleep, because he said he had heard wolves howling in the distance. Well, nobody knows how distant the wolves actually were.

Before the last gig, both Mike and me knew it was the end. None of the other guys knew, and I don't remember if we told them before or after the gig. I just knew that it would be the last show. There was a big crowd, and I wondered if it would feel special, but it didn't. The gig was a downer.

Okay, then, before the Polish tour we had also played the Razzle memorial gigs when Sami was still in the band. Actually I consider those the real last Hanoi gigs. The memorial shows took place in Kulttuuritalo, Helsinki, at home in Finland, and they were nice. It still felt good to play. Terry Chimes was a really good drummer, especially knowing he had only rehearsed for a week. The Polish tour was something we should never have done. If we had quit after Kulttuuritalo, I would have mostly good memories from Hanoi Rocks.

Looking back, Hanoi Rocks was a huge influence for rock 'n' roll bands around the world. It's pretty crazy. We didn't plan it, we just figured everything would be okay as long as we could make a living, but it became such a huge thing, something that's still big news all over the world. Hanoi Rocks has often been called a legendary band, and that's something I'm really proud of. Especially because all the original members are still alive. I love them all.

Michael on tour.

From Poland we flew back to London, where everybody went their own way. Sami and Anna moved to Stockholm, and Sami wound up being a stay-at-home dad until he was asked to join a band called Jetboy. That took him back to Los Angeles, and after leaving Jetboy he moved to New York and played with Mike Monroe for a couple of years, but that wasn't really happening either. To my knowledge, he's happy now. He has a band with his wife, Carmen, who I guess is a real nice girl, because their thing has lasted so long. Sami finally found his true love. Let's hope it lasts. He had been searching for it for at least fifteen years.

Nasse studied to be a pharmacist. After Hanoi broke up, Nasse and me still continued in the same band. His first marriage went on the rocks. His wife was called Simone, but the roadies called her "She-moans." Fuck, she was a bad choice. I wouldn't have touched her with a ten-foot pole even if we had been the last two people on earth. That girl was just so full of shit. Then Nasse fell in love with a Finnish woman called Tiina and got married. They first lived in Japan because Tiina was working there. Nasse has completely distanced himself from drugs, and that's just great.

Gyp Casino, our original drummer, works at a record shop in Stockholm. I guess he's the manager. Mike has been gigging with his own band. He's had all these different bands. He lives in Turku, Finland. He did some solo stuff in the States that didn't do so great commercially. I think it's because of his weakness: He needs somebody else to write with. Mike's talent lies elsewhere; he's a multi-instrumentalist and a great arranger. Razzle is in heaven. For me, he was a part of that phase in my life when boys turn to men.

AFTER HANOI BROKE UP, I wondered what to do next. Me and Nasse figured we'd try something different, and got a band going with a girl singer, and that became Cherry Bombz. We got Terry Chimes on drums, and at first my old guitar tech Timo Kaltio was on bass, but he was soon replaced by Dave Tregunna. I stole Dave from the Lords of the New Church, which meant the death of that band. Yeah, I killed them along the way, too.

We soon ran into trouble with our singer, Anita Chellemah. We had a one-night stand once, just a drunken mistake, but afterwards we really began to clash. We were fighting just all the time. First everything was okay, but the more we toured, the more her drinking began to annoy me. Anita began her day with a bottle of wine. She had the habit of opening a wine bottle by standing on top of it and pushing the cork down with the heel of her shoe. Gulp and go.

CAPITAL PUNISHMENT • I really don't know if I'm in favor of death penalty. Well, I guess I'm not, not at the moment, anyway. Of course it depends on what you've done. If you've killed ten thousand men and women and children and your troops have raped two thousand women, I guess Trio Niskalaukaus ("a shot in the neck") might cure you. I don't know what's worse: to subject somebody to that band's music night and day, or shoot them three times in the neck. You can surely kill a person both ways.

Our last gig was at the Cat Club in New York. It was totally packed, and Anita got drunk before the gig. We were supposed to sign a contract the following day. It was a fuckin' mess. She fell off the stage during the gig, and when she tried to climb back, security thought she was a crazy fan and threw her out. After the gig, a punch-fest ensued. Billy Idol was there with his father, and they had to watch that shit go down. When Anita managed to get back inside after the gig, she just glared at me like an angry tiger, and then in a second, she was on top of me. These girls really know how to fight, and when they explode, oh man! They're dangerous, and this girl was especially dangerous.

I had had enough. Cherry Bombz was a really good band, but we were stuck touring the States, and I also believe that people were expecting something harder from me after Hanoi.

Cherry Bombz was a pop band, a good pop band, but it was neither the time nor place for it.

When Cherry Bombz broke up, I thought of making a solo LP. At that point, I developed a pretty nasty heroin habit, so the recordings were a bit of a mess. I left some mistakes in the final mix. I could hear the screwups but I just didn't care. Somehow I had lost the will to do any kind of music, so I had to take a break. After finishing the album I went back to the U.K., but then, wondering what the hell was I doing there, I'd just spend my time doing dope. I ended up going back to the States to kick the habit over there.

Me, Anastasia, and Sebastian flew to the U.S. and got a place in Orange County, where I managed to clean myself up. I also got new management, Anita Camarata and Danny Goldberg, and hired David Codikow as my lawyer. It was nice to meet up with Sami in L.A. Some other Helsinki guys were around, too; Rane from Smack had stayed behind after some gig. I guess their band had broken up in L.A. I wrote some new songs, and we started shopping for a deal.

I had to sign a new contract with Virgin because Hanoi had split up, and I also got rid of my publishing deal with Zomba. The Virgin deal meant money and a house in Venice, but my relationship with Stacy was very strained. You gotta remember that I met Stacy when I was twenty-one or twenty-two and she was thirty-three. The age difference was starting to show. I occasionally partied in Hollywood with friends like Steve Jones. We talked with Lenny Kravitz about forming a band, but nothing came of it. The same thing with a lot of other people, too. Nothing ever resulted from those talks.

122

VII

I got a call that Iggy Pop wanted to meet me. Iggy was about to go on tour. Steve Jones couldn't make it for some reason, so he had recommended me to play guitar. I met Iggy, and he was a real nice guy, a gentleman. We hung out for a day, me just strumming on the acoustic, and we decided to do it together. The tour ended up lasting fifteen months, including rehearsals and all that. We were on the road for seven months, but my gig lasted longer.

First we picked the guys for the band. Iggy said he knew a fuckin' great drummer from New York called Paul Garisto—he had played on Iggy's last LP—and I thought that Alvin Gibbs, my pal from the U.K. Subs, would be an ideal bass player. I knew he was already way more into Iggy's stuff than I was. Then we decided to have Seamus Beaghe from Madness on keyboards. My job was to come up with live arrangements for the songs. Shit, the list was long as fuck, maybe forty songs altogether, and I wondered how I would be able to wade through 'em all. Then the rest of the band arrived in town, and we had a couple of days to get acquainted and stuff.

The chief roadies and our tour manager showed up, and we started rehearsing the set. The pace was roughly the same as in Hanoi. Maybe not as hard, but pretty close: five days a week, six to eight hours a day. We decided to have a warm-up gig in some small town in California, somewhere like Santa Barbara, and it clicked instantly. I had the same feeling I had in Hanoi when Razzle was still alive: This band kicks ass. Some twenty gigs later, Iggy's band was a well-oiled, mean machine, and we took that machine all around the world. On that tour we went to all the places I still hadn't been.

We began with some club dates in the States, immediately followed by a tour in bigger venues. We partied, and of course there were chicks. I made real good money, and my wages were paid straight to my account. To my misfortune I was still married to Anastasia, although we didn't sleep in the same bed anymore, and she had full access to my bank account, because I hadn't done anything about it. Of course somebody had to pay the rent, and I wanted to make sure she and Sebastian had enough money to live, but I should have asked somebody else to oversee my account. Something really shitty happened because of that, but I'll get back to that later.

While touring Europe we wound up in Berlin in the middle of winter. It was about 5°F when we played in this fuckin' circus tent. Okay, when you're onstage and you have all the lights and you move around, you'll thaw pretty quickly, but

before the gig we were all standing there in our T-shirts and shivering like fuck. It was really sick. London was nice because I had the chance to meet up with old friends. And Iggy—oh man. As soon as his wife Suchi, whom he later divorced, had flown back to

THE ROAD OF THE ROMANIS • Just think about the whole trip from India to Finland, Europe, how long it has taken. Goddamn, it's been a long journey. I guess it took about a thousand years for the Gypsy people to get here, because they had to work along the way to get food and everything. That's nomadic life.

New York, Iggy just had to get some. He's not able to see for shit without his glasses, and there was this horrible groupie in a red leotard. Our hotel room windows were sort of parallel to Iggy's room, so we had a real live show when Iggy was banging that broad in his room. His ass moved in such a furious tempo that any rabbit would've been jealous.

Miami. We had a couple days off in Florida. Hot, moist, and expensive. Iggy scored some blow and whispered: "I bought some coke, let's go to the bathroom." He hacked himself a big, fat line, snorted it like a vacuum cleaner, and screamed: "Iggy's back!"

We took the limo back to Orlando—or was it Fort Lauderdale? Anyway, our headquarters in Florida. We always tried to stay in the same hotel as long as possible and drive back and forth to the gigs. Iggy was constantly snorting lines on the backseat of a stretch limo. His wife looked at me like she wanted to murder me, as if I had bought that coke. On the same night, I met some bikini chick, who came to have a couple of drinks in my room—we had nothing more than that going on. After a while, there was a knock on the door. Iggy.

"Do you have any booze? Do you have any booze?"

I had a bottle of cognac, but basically Iggy just wanted to calm down. Because we had no Valium or anything, it just couldn't work. A bit later there was another knock on the door, and this time it was the rest of the band. Everybody was high as a kite.

Alvin Gibbs, the bass player, later wrote a whole book about the tour called *Neighborhood Threat: On Tour With Iggy Pop.* Lots of critics wondered in their reviews how come it's called *On Tour With Iggy,* because 75 percent of the book is about me. All through the book Alvin underlines how everybody else had girls but not him, and that's total bullshit. He had some chicks too, all right. According to the book, I was the root of all evil, but the other band members had their part in it, too. Naturally, I did party every once in a while.

I think the nicest leg of the tour was Australia, where I met this old model friend of mine who had landed a gig in Sydney. We were just hanging out, but the rest of the guys freaked out: "How can you fuckin' know all these beautiful women all around the world?" Obviously they just didn't know about the trail of pussy I had gone through in my younger days. But we just hung out with that model chick. It was the only time during that tour we even touched heroin: We shelled out forty bucks and got this big Chinese rock. We snorted it with most of the band members and a couple of model girls, and it was really potent stuff. Afterwards we just nodded, took walks, went to clubs.

I like the vibe in Australia in general. It's somewhere between the U.K. and the U.S., but much more relaxed than in the U.S. They don't have gun mania over there in Australia. It's definitely one of the nicest places I've ever toured. Of course, there are these exotic places, too. But for instance New Zealand was pretty much boredom for me. I mean, a couple million people and a couple million sheep—yeah, right.

Andy in Tokyo on the Iggy tour.

In Japan it was a bit embarrassing when the crowd shouted my name louder than the band could play. I had to tell the audience like, "Hey, I'm here with Iggy Pop, give the man due respect and enjoy the gig." Only then did they calm down. The rest of the band were flabbergasted when they realized how big I was in Japan, and saw how many gifts I received from the fans. I had people from my own Japanese label taking care of me day and night, and they chauffeured me to interviews and drove me all around the city. Hey, it was interesting anyway.

Iggy Pop is a wonderful guy, but he's really unsure about himself. He has horrible stage fright. When he got offstage, he used to moan about not being good enough. He set such high standards for himself. In my opinion, he's one of the best and most underrated vocalists, from the '60s to this day. Only Michael, Jagger, and maybe Tyler, are in the same league. I met David Bowie through Iggy. David used to hang out pretty often at the time. He's another true gentleman—and a ladykiller. He was eyeballing every chick, like, "Check that out!" Goddamn, that guy was like me when I was twenty.

But then it was time for Bowie to go back to New York and for us to head to South America. We did South America before Europe, and the first stop was São Paulo, Brazil. The city was dirty as fuck and endlessly vast. In the first hotel, Jim—that's Iggy—threw a tantrum. He kicked over furniture and yelled: "We came to play from the fuckin' other side of the world, and you try to put us into this roach motel!" After a shouting match, a new hotel was found. I had my fists up, too, alongside Jim.

There was not much nightlife in São Paulo, but I managed to find a rockabilly club. It was crazy to see all these guys in drapes and creepers and beautiful Latina girls in their ponytails and '50s skirts dancing to old hits by Little Richard and the others. Free beer kept on flowing, and there was no way I could have smoked all the weed on offer. Our own venue was a big, gloomy hall, but the crowd went apeshit and just slammed, screamed, and stage-dived like there was no tomorrow. The band had become a killing machine.

Next day we flew to Rio de Janeiro, where me and Jim went to hang out on the beach. We were chillin' out when this guy suddenly pulls off Jim's Nike sneakers and runs away. Jim looks at me and says, "Andy, do something," but I just laughed. The guy already had a five-hundred-yard lead. I would never have caught him. In Rio, some of the other guys in the band got really amped on coke, but I said no.

We spent the next night doing interviews. When we got back to the hotel, I decided to get acquainted with the local street urchins. I took a bottle of cognac, found a nice side alley, and within fifteen minutes I had seven new friends, all homeless throwaways. They told me the places to go and places to avoid in Rio. One of the guys told me he had only one dream: Europe. Over there, the American dream had already died. My new friends said the U.S. helped the rich, not the poor. Fuck, man.

We played two shows in Rio and continued to Uruguay and Argentina. Buenos Aires is a charming city. People were beautiful and we played a killer gig. As usual, after the gig we first went back to the hotel and had dinner after a while. That night Paul Garisto the drummer and me went to the strangest party I've ever seen in my life. There were about fifteen or twenty people in two rooms, and the weirdest thing was that nobody said a word to each other. Each person had something like fifteen to thirty grams of coke in front of them, and they just sat in silence and snorted the stuff. I mean, coke is supposed to be a social booster, and just a small hit will usually turn you into a motormouth even if you don't feel like talking. The party was a real downer for me as well as for Paul. We managed to hail a cab and went back to the hotel to sleep.

By then, Henry McGroggan, our tour manager, figured out that if he wrote down the name of the hotel on everybody's arm with magic marker, he could be sure that everybody was there—at least by morning, when it was time to go.

Sometimes I was also a good boy. I'd order a bottle of red and a plate of cheese and have the bellhop spread some candles around the room. Then I'd take a hot bath, drink the wine, eat the cheese, and relax, wondering if me and Angela would become an item. This was just before we got together. I'd also wonder what my dear mother was up to, and my sister, brother, all my friends in Europe. And then I'd sleep like a log.

From South America we flew back to New York, where I hung out with Iggy for a while. We were preparing for Europe. In the meantime, I taught him some basic guitar chords. First up was the U.K.—all sold-out shows, lots of TV and interviews. At that point the interviewers usually requested Iggy and me, or Iggy, or me. A hierarchy had formed: There were the stars, Iggy and Andy, and the band, Alvin, Seamus, and Paul.

I realized not everybody can stand that kind of life. Some people began throwing useless tantrums for no apparent reason. They just wanted some attention. But that's not how the world works. You gotta earn the respect; you'll never get it by bawling like a baby. It all comes down to working hard, learning, working some more, and respecting others. I've sometimes seen these young bucks give their roadies a hard time, and I wonder if they ever heard the wisdom: "If the roadies don't roll, the band can't rock"?

After the U.K. came time for the rest of Europe. In Copenhagen I met an old lady friend of mine, and we spent the next four or five days together. I'm sure you'll guess what we did when I was not onstage. Then I continued to Germany and she stayed in Copenhagen. We also played a killer show in Stockholm. My sister came to see us and really liked it, and we got rave reviews in all the papers: "If you no longer believe in rock 'n' roll, go check out Iggy and Andy!" The band had definitely become that good.

The Suicide Twins. My acoustic project. A fiasco. Four years before everybody started raving about the unplugged thing. Once again I was too far ahead.

I remembered all those weeks I spent polishing and rearranging Iggy's songs before the tour. Everything had seemed so distant then, but now I had the feeling that all the effort had been worthwhile. Iggy had never played "Johanna" or "Penetration" live before, for instance. Rearranging the songs was pretty boring, but that's when I understood why you gotta have a live arrangement. On the album the songs have a different purpose altogether. Iggy knew I understood the live dynamics, so he gave me free rein to choose and arrange the songs.

I think we then did the Netherlands, Belgium (the most boring place in the world), Germany, Switzerland, and Greece. On our first night in Greece they prepared a wonderful traditional Greek dinner for us: Wine and ouzo flowed, the air was thick with weed smoke, and the food was top-notch. Paul even managed to pick up a Greek beauty that night while the rest of us were sound asleep.

I dreamed about when we used to play cowboys and Indians as kids. In the dream, I remembered the time I shot an arrow at my opponent, and of course it hit him straight in the eye. The poor boy was hurt badly, but a four- or five-year-old kid can't really understand that he has hurt somebody. It was just a game. Naturally, I was once again seriously rebuked at home.

Well, enough of my dreams. The Athens gig was at this football stadium, and man, it was a killer show. To quote Michael Monroe: "We rocked like fuck!" So did the audience, goddammit, they really knew how to party. It's really important to have the feedback between the artist and the audience. You have to get the crowd going and make them feel good, and they will give it back to you. But because there are more of them, that energy must be ten times or a hundred times more powerful before you can send it back to them with your music. And then it just grows and grows until it's in full bloom, and becomes an extreme high for both the audience and the artist. I guess it's some kind of nirvana. Even an orgasm or a shot of pure Thai smack can never beat that feeling. It's a 100 percent natural high. Hey, isn't that enough reason to wonder why you should dabble with chemicals at all? At least it is for me. Sex is

Razzle had just joined Hanoi. London, circa '83.

Next to some pub.

different, because it's an intimate thing between two people (or more, depending on the situation—sure, I've been to bed with three chicks. I just had the feeling there were two people too many).

But back to the audience, the fans. They're all around the world and I love 'em all. Without their support, I guess I wouldn't have made it through the hard times. They've given me diamonds, gold wristlets, platinum wristlets, awesome rags, et cetera. I thank each and everyone of you. How could I ever forget? There's a Gypsy *calo* heart beating in my chest, and it's full of honor. Thank you, all who believed in me while I was living in heroin hell. And you who came to offer me more, you're really asking for it.

Anyway, the following morning, an extremely hungover band appeared in the hotel lobby. Next up was Israel. (Yikes, poor Israel! If you only knew.)

WHEN THE PLANE LANDED, we were surprisingly met by the same promoter who had organized the Hanoi gigs in Israel. He turned pale and stuttered: "That, that, that guy again!" Well, there was an explanation. We had been in Israel with Hanoi. I can just blame Nasty for the fact that the promoter went into a panic after seeing me. It's actually pretty simple, in a way: Everybody recognizes the monkey, but the monkey recognizes no one.

You see, we rehearsed in Israel for a Hanoi world tour, and kept pretty colorful company. There were some British journos, friends, et cetera. During the day, we rehearsed the *Back to Mystery City* live set, and each night we played a gig and partied like crazy. I got bored with the chicks pretty fast, and after two nights I just tried to shove my Arab bunny off onto Nasty, Sammy, Razzle, or just anybody from our crew. She just kept saying, "I be woman of one man." Well, I tried to avoid her, and kept on drinking and smoking pot with everyone.

We rehearsed at this club. On the third day the owner showed up and tried to give us some shit, but we were having none of it. Our contract stated that drinks would be free. In three days, our entourage had managed to drink $15,000 worth of the liquid drug. The guy asked, pleaded, even begged that we pay for at least half of the drinks. No way, man.

Some other things got out of hand too. The super freaks of Tel Aviv began packing our gigs, and we cracked jokes about them in between songs, although we still played like true professionals. One night we decided we'd have a party in Nasse's room. We spread the word at the club that there would be a party the next night in room so-and-so. When the party began, between sixty and eighty people were in the two-room minisuite. Nasse and me got a bit carried away during the night. There were some broken windows, and somehow the wallpaper got torn off.

At 5:25 AM I realized I was sitting on the bed. I could see Razzle's head half-buried under torn wallpaper and broken glass. It looked almost if he had constructed a bunk for himself.

Like, "It's warm under this stuff, I won't get chilly." Then I noticed I had a golden retriever puppy in my lap. She was sweet as can be, maybe three months old. Then I turned my head and saw something much more disturbing. Our beloved Wolf of Sipoo, Nasty, is industriously trying to push this cast-iron garden table over the balcony railing. He had fallen down the stairs of a London nightclub before we came to Israel, and so had a cast on his leg. The table began to rise.

KIRSI KOSKINEN

Building on tradition, Stockholm '94.

Live Ammo = Dan Lagerstedt, Angela, Andy, Gyp Casino.

Slowly and surely it tipped upward. This I gotta see, I thought. The table was almost on the railing, it began to tilt, soon it was on the other side, and then—bombs away.

If you don't know, I can tell you that on weekdays, Tel Aviv is totally dead from 1 AM to 6:30 AM But just as the table was about to hit the ground, a cab appeared out of nowhere and the table crashed into the cab. It went right through the roof and smashed into the backseat. Fortunately there was only the driver in the car, because even an idiot could see that a passenger would've been instantly killed. Luckily the cab was empty.

I sat down, knowing that pretty soon it was going to be pandemonium. Knock, knock, knock. I took a gulp of Rémy Martin. Nasse stumbled over Razzle and opened the door. The hotel manager screamed in broken English: "Where band manager? Where band manager?" After a while he managed to cut his foot on the broken glass littering the room. He continued to scream, and of course he soon cuts his other foot, too. It started to get really funny with him jumping from one foot to another, but then Nasty had finally had it. BANG, BONG, he hit the hotel manager in the head with his crutch.

The poor guy ran away and so did I, because I didn't wanna be there when the cops arrived. I fled to my own suite, and there me and my adopted puppy decided to hide in the closet. I passed out and woke up when six uniformed guys, looking tough as nails and carrying Uzis and an AK-47, dragged me out with our friend, the hotel manager. So that's what happened the last time we were in Israel.

Thank God corruption still does the trick in places like

137

that. And thank God for the £50,000 CBS sent us later on. Neither me nor Nasse got attempted murder or assault charges on our asses.

So after all it was no wonder that the promoter got nervous when he saw me with Iggy. But if he had any fears, they soon dissipated. I acted like a total gentleman, not like a snotty kid anymore. We played a killer gig in Israel, and I also got to meet the late Ofra Haza. I had been a big fan of hers for years. How beautiful and nice this Yemenite woman was. Rest in peace.

On Christmas I flew back to Los Angeles. It was a luxury to be the only passenger aboard a 757. The twelve stewardesses and me just drank, partied, slept, and drank some more until the captain announced: "We're landing in Los Angeles. Please fasten your seat belts—and Andy, thank you for the privilege of flying you here!" I had given him a bunch of CDs during the flight.

During the final dates in Australia the band turned against Iggy. They had some ridiculous demands to get more money. I wouldn't take part in it, because there's no sense in killing a friendship over money. No thanks to that.

And that was it for the Iggy tour. I returned to Los Angeles, and you already know what happened to the money I made.

Stacy was too old to be my wife, but Angela was the same age as me. We liked the same bands and shared the same kind of past. We've now been married for twelve years, and I've never cheated on her. There's no need to, because she gives me everything a guy could ever want.

~ VIII ~

We, Angela and I, decided to go to Europe in '94, when there was a really bad earthquake in California, 7.7 on the Richter scale. We thought maybe it would be safer in Europe. During the earthquake I really thought my time had come. I was like, "Sorry, God. If I screwed it up, please forgive me." I guess I prayed for Angela too. She told me that later.

I called Tiina Vuorinen to hook me up with something in Finland. In the summer of 1994, I toured Finland under the name Shooting Gallery, but the choice of singer was Tiina Vuorinen's biggest mistake. Tiina has been a great help along the years, but that was a major screwup. Man, that guy was a fuckin' clown! He couldn't dress, he couldn't speak. *"No Inglese!"* Or *"Poquito."* His ass was black and blue because me, Angela, or Danny Lagerstedt would kick him each time he fucked up. Then I recorded *Building on Tradition.* That got me the number one single "Strung Out" in Finland. It was the kind of stuff that Hanoi would've probably done if we had continued, but these dunderheads just couldn't sell records outside Finland. Too bad.

This album would've killed everything Hanoi ever did. We didn't even shoot a video until "Strung Out" was at the top of the charts. Yeah, welcome to Europe, Andy.

But Europe has been okay. They made a movie of me called *The Real McCoy*. It's pretty interesting to watch now, because the shooting started just before I quit using heroin for good. It was an interesting experience in other respects, too. I had never seen how they actually make a movie. Fortunately, my wife co-starred in the film, because she teaches Method acting. Without her, I'd never have made it—I mean, how can you suddenly just cry or laugh on cue? Angela was a tremendous help, and she should have gotten much more credit for that.

It was directed by a guy called Pekka Lehto, who became a pretty good friend of mine. We would just sit down, I would tell him stories, and he would decide which ones would be filmed. Almost the whole movie was based on my ideas, so it was a shock when the movie came out and the screenplay was credited to some girl. That's almost stealing: Somebody has all these ideas but someone else takes the credit, as if she had come up with everything herself. I was pretty baffled, man. When it comes to my financial agreements with Pekka, I really have no comment. Pekka is a really nice guy, but also pretty idealistic—the kind of guy who probably belonged to the Communist Party in the '60s and '70s.

But hey, the movie turned out nice and became really popular. It was also a real trip to visit the Bollywood studios in Bombay, truly a wonderful experience. I had previously visited Universal and MGM studios in the U.S., but they didn't come close to the Indian studios: They had complete replicas of Piccadilly Circus, Times Square, all kinds of places there, and it really was like nothing I'd ever seen. And everything worked like a clock. Everybody knew what they were doing.

It was also great to take part in the screening of *The Real McCoy* at the Berlin International Film Festival. For the first time in the history of the festival, all the critics, about three thousand of 'em, rose up and applauded. That was pretty unbelievable. I would have never believed I'd see them give a standing ovation. Hey, that was a new experience too.

One hilarious thing about making the movie was when I called Mike and asked if he wanted to be in it too. Mike agreed. He had found this old deserted house near his summer place, and in the movie that hovel is supposed to be Mike's home. I walk in and say, "Wow, you've invested your money in a real palace!" Afterwards people came to ask me if it really was Mike's house.

Like, "It sure could use a new paint job or something!" I can only laugh behind their backs—hey, no way, you dunderheads. That's pretty rich.

We were supposed to be done with the shooting in six months. "Give or take an hour," Pekka said, "it's all there. We're gonna finish it in six months." About four years later, I noticed that we were still shooting. That's when I began to think that Pekka Lehto, our beloved director, had gone totally bonkers. I started to see my future before my eyes like a film, and it felt like somebody just kept on yelling: "No, cut, we'll have another take!" I was surrounded by cameras all the time. You could've made a TV series out of the material we shot, because there was just so much of it. Although some of it was pretty sick.

Katakali dancer. Southern India, spring '97.

There was some juicy stuff that wasn't filmed. I had a bad accident where I fell from a fourth-story balcony, landed on concrete, and broke both legs in numerous places. I had to sit in a wheelchair for a long time. As soon as I got out of the chair, I called my mom and told her that I didn't need the chair any more. "Oh, how nice," she said.

The next morning about 6 AM my mom was on her way to work while we were filming on Senaatintori. In the finale of

142

the movie I receive the keys to the Kingdom of Heaven from St. Peter on the roof of the Suurkirkko church—there's this statue of St. Peter holding the keys up on the roof. As my mother passed Senaatintori on her way to work, she saw my stunt man climbing high on the roof of the church. She almost had a stroke: "Oh my, that's Andy on the roof! Now he's gone totally funny in the head!" Of course, she couldn't know that it was just my double who had been made up to look like me. "There goes my crazy son again," my mother thought. "Oh my, oh my, I guess therapy is the only answer to his problems now!"

In the meantime, Angela and me lived in India for almost a year. It was a time of love in paradise: We lay on beaches, went on jungle expeditions, and hung out with other travelers and local friends. Our house had six bedrooms and two living

Angela and Andy painted with some extra

baggage and blue eyes in true Bollywood style, '97.

Surrealistic commune, Kerala, India, '97.

rooms, and in the garden the trees bore pineapples, coconuts, mangoes, and papayas. Angela got a perfect tan and I wrote new songs. I guess some of them will eventually be recorded.

Angela and me also spent time in southern Thailand in another paradiselike environment, diving among fish of a million different colors and making love. We said to each other we're surely going to have a child, because what else could be God's will? If not a little Chad, then little Sarah, God willing. In thirty-eight years, life has given me more than most people could experience in about ten incarnations. That's a blessing.

Another blessing was this one Finnish tour when I brought along my pianist friend Nicky Hopkins, who had played on John Lennon's "Imagine," some Beatles songs, and on "Angie" and "Wild Horses" by the Stones. Dave Lindholm came along too, and it was great that I could introduce Dave to my friends.

Nicky and Dave became good pals, and that warmed my heart. They instantly got on well, like a house on fire. It was a great tour, and even I had to smile while standing on the side of the stage with Angela, watching during Dave's set.

What's so interesting about me, guys?
An Indian pig, '96.

On a beach in southern Thailand.

146
— SHERIFF —

IX

My relationship with Mike is deep as hell, and sometimes difficult. We were so very young when we met. We originally bumped into each other at the Töölö church where we were both rehearsing. It turned out that ultimately we both had the same goal: to form the best rock 'n' roll band in the world. It meant five years of hard work for us.

You gotta remember that we were thirteen years old when the dream began. I had moved away from Roy, and first I suggested that we should get him from Stockholm to play rhythm guitar. Mike was all for it, but for some reason nothing came of it. Somehow it just didn't work out. Roy wanted to play soul and reggae, and we wanted to play rock 'n' roll. At the time, rock 'n' roll was pretty fuckin' scarce, so we wanted to write rock 'n' roll songs. We were both still really inexperienced. Sometimes we lived in Stockholm, sometimes in Helsinki. We both quit school too fuckin' early, of course.

In Stockholm we had a band called Nymphomaniacs. I guess we never played a single show. Mike had this doctor's

Briard Revisited. From left: Angela, Pete Malmi, Andy, Jussi 69, Archzie.

coat, stolen from some hospital, and I had drawn our logo on the back. It was an erect dick, I mean, the male organ in all its glory, just about to come. Sperm was spurting out, and our name exploded out of the sperm: the Nymphomaniacs! But basically that band was more about attitude than music.

Punk had been a revelation to us, all these new bands like the Ruts and the Damned. We were also starting to get into political reggae, acid soul, and bands like Undisputed Truth. I introduced Mike to some of that stuff, and Mike introduced me to hard rock, as I wasn't too familiar with that scene, I mean the metal stuff. I never listened to bands like Led Zeppelin, but Mike had a huge collection of their bootlegs. I gotta admit that Jimmy Page was a fuckin' great guitarist in his heyday. Afterwards he got boring. Robert Plant later had a really beautiful single called "Big Log," very Spanish-influenced musically.

We had been talking about getting Nasse in the band. We gave him the name "Suicide" that I originally used in Briard. I had become McCoy when our first single came out. I was in Stockholm at the time, and when they asked what name they should use for the cover, Pete Malmi said: "Real McCoy—that's what he is, the real stuff." And I've been McCoy ever since. All I have is my name. Over the years I adopted it in my private life, too. In the beginning Dave Lindholm and Albert Jarvinen really helped me out. They really encouraged me, and had no stupid illusions that I would be trespassing on their turf or anything.

Yeah, we had some weird times in Hanoi. Afterwards I didn't work with Mike for many years. Somehow we totally lost the connection. I don't know if it was the managers who tried to keep us apart. The managers thought I was really valuable— Mike was the face of the band, but I had the gift of writing songs, and that gift has just developed over the years. Dunno, but I guess the drugs also had a big part in the split. I think we decided before the last Polish tour that we would just call it

All night with the lights on. Michael and Stiv Bators, Notting Hill, London '83.

JON BLACKMORE, *MELODY MAKER*

a day. The new guys were just awful. I really don't know who picked them out, but it wasn't me. I was in Sri Lanka.

When the Hanoi Rocks box set came out, Mike asked me to come to Turku, Finland, to do some interviews. Okay, I saw there had been some changes over the years. I noticed that for the first time, Mike was in control of his own life and nobody was whispering in his ear what he should or shouldn't do. At the press conference, Mike said he would play a couple songs that evening before this Swedish band came on, and he asked me to come along. Of course I would always play with Mike, because it's nice to be onstage with him. We did a couple of songs, and it was a gas. It really rocked, so we thought we should meet more often, and suddenly the new songs started coming. Mike is a creative guy and his talent complements my own. It's not just a stage thing but something bigger, something that just gels. It's also very much to do with how we write songs together.

The blond beast and the
brown-haired beast.
Hanoi box set release party.

I think Mike is a multi-instrumentalist genius. Maybe not the best writer in the world, but hey, I'm not the best multi-instrumentalist in the world. I know how to write, so the balance is really good. We have taken just one day at a time and written some songs. Hopefully there will be an album one day.

Of course it's different to work with Mike again. The last time we worked together I was deep in my private drug hell, so occupied with my heroin habit that I didn't necessarily let anyone close. The only thing I was interested in was getting high and just sitting alone in the room. I was pretty antisocial. And the one thing that amazes me is how somebody who drinks alcohol can condemn smoking hash and call it a drug. Isn't anything that messes up your head a drug? Alcohol, heroin, opium, whatever, even cocaine. But now it's all behind me. Mike and me realized that everything worked better these days, so we decided to do the Ruisrock festival.

Backstage photo: Helsinki rockers in 2001. Dave, Andy, Ville, and Michael.

KIRSI KOSKINEN

Of course, just before our Ruisrock gig some drunken fuckin' idiots jumped my guitar tech, and his shoulder was dislocated. Thank you so much for preventing the man from doing his job. I happened to see my American friend Ricky there, Ricky London, and he tried to take care of the guitars, but it just didn't work out the way it was supposed to. At least the guy tried. The sound on stage was so chaotic that I couldn't even hear if I was out of tune. Nothing is as horrible as playing a guitar that's out of tune, or listening to a guitar that's out of tune. Well, people had to put up with that for about three songs at Ruisrock. The worst thing was that this other guy, who's a guitarist himself, left all my guitars in the sun. It's plain awful when a couple of strings are out of tune. The whole song is in shambles, and it all sounds like a big echo chamber where seventeen drunken priests are squalling and hollering as they're falling into the fiery pits of hell.

I BELIEVE WHAT MADE HANOI ROCKS THE MOST SUCCESSFUL and influential Finnish band ever was the magic of Mike and me

Rocking out with Mr. Monroe
at Ruisrock 2001.

Alive and still climbing up.
Michael at the first
Hanoi Revisited gig.

153

YEAH! It's only r 'n' r, 'n' I love it!

together. I think the magic comes from something karmic that happened in our past lives. When everything clicks, we're a well-oiled machine, even if we haven't seen each other for years, as we proved in Turku before the Hellacopters went on. If there is no balance, everything goes straight to hell. I'm a Libra, that's my thing. Mike is Gemini, and Geminis are obviously two-faced—hey, that's a joke, but they can really have two opinions about the same thing, which can also be a positive thing. I believe there's something in horoscopes, and I believe there will always be a connection between Mike and me for the rest of our lives, even if we don't play in the same band. It's something we started when we were young, and we have to do it all the way. I believe it really doesn't matter anymore whether we retire together or separately. Of course it would be nice to quit when we're old as shit. That's what I hope, at least.

RUISROCK • We used as many fireworks as the Stones did and arrived in a helicopter. I hope that was not to be my last flight, if you know what I mean.

Mike had a terrible loss just a while ago. We all lost a close, dear friend. I met her at the same time as Mike when she worked as an A&R rep at the Epic/CBS headquarters in New York. She was supposed to do our press for the last U.S. tour. She was just so full of life, she always smiled and made everybody feel good. She put her career at stake for Hanoi Rocks. She was called Jude Wilder. As recognition for her work, Mike thanked Jude at our first gig in New York by dedicating "Don't You Ever Leave Me" to her. I almost feel like it was an omen, a portent of what was to come. I don't wanna be an old lady and go into details of how and why they got together, but hey, when two people fall in love, it's meant to be. And that was meant to be.

The sudden death of Jude has been a shock for us all, especially because Mike, Jude, and me were together that same morning. Of course we all later blamed ourselves for one thing or another, but hey, maybe it was better this way. At least she left peacefully. She had a sister who was waiting for her on the other side, I know that. But it caused such great pain for Mike. If I could carry only 10 percent of it, or 20 percent, I would be ready to carry half of it—I couldn't carry it all alone—I would do it. But that's impossible. And that's a sign of friendship.

I've only had two real friends in my life. The other was Roy Hamilton, who died much too young, and goddammit, if that happened to Mike, I couldn't live anymore. I would have no air to breathe. Mike has gone through real hard times, but he has shown me that he has a hundred times more guts than most of the guys I see—these guys who are still doing smack although I quit six years ago myself. They've been in and out of jail, and they just can't see they're going nowhere. What surprises me even more is that after doing time for hard drugs, the first thing they wanna do when they get out is to get high. I don't know, I've been behind bars myself, as they say, and when you get out, you're screaming for vengeance. Like, "I'm gonna avenge myself on society, I'll get high, fuck you all!" But the only revenge is on you—you just sink into that same old drug shit again.

When I look back on what Hanoi Rocks has accomplished, I can be proud. I'm especially proud of these two small kids, this dark-haired boy from East Helsinki who was called just Andy back then, and a kid who lived on Sibeliuksenkatu whose name

Michael, Jude, Andy, and Angela.

was Mike, Mike Monroe. It's been a while since we sat on bus number 16, thinking up a name for our band. Johnny Thunders' *L.A.M.F.*, "Like a Mother Fucker," had just come out, and it had a song about heroin called "Chinese Rocks." I had also seen a movie where they talked about "Hanoi rocks," heroin produced in Hanoi. I thought if that wasn't a cool name for a band, I knew nothing about anything. "What about Hanoi Rocks?" I asked. Mike was: "Fuck! There it is!" So there it was.

Hanoi Rocks has become a worldwide cult. It's hard to beat our track record. You just gotta tour and tour. I've noticed so many times that wherever I go in the world, I'm recognized. I have no privacy. Has it been worth it? I think it's been worth every fuckin' second. It's fantastic when people from all over the world thank me for a certain song. When I wrote that song, maybe in a tiny one-room apartment on Karlaplan, Stockholm, I would've never expected that someone on the other side of the world would love it and plaster the walls of his or her room with my pictures. I can never thank my fans enough, man.

I believe Hanoi Rocks never let down their fans, and

that's still honored starting with Hanoi Revisited. That's how the current thing with Mike started. We're gonna start using the name Monroe-McCoy. Alphabetically it should be McCoy-Monroe, but it's stupid if the guitarist's name is before the singer. C'mon, there are some traditions you gotta respect.

I'VE NOW PLAYED ALL MY LIFE, and I've spent the past twenty years, since I was eighteen, learning this business inside out and outside in. The first thing I gotta warn young musicians about is that you should never sign a publishing deal and a recording deal with the same label. In the publishing deal, you sign away your rights for your own songs.

It used to be the custom in Finland that the label people were like, "Oh, you wanna make an album, okay, you need to sign this publishing deal that goes along with it. Here, have some advance money." These young guys who have never seen any money just sell away their rights, all these so-called mechanical royalties for radio play, jukebox play, et cetera. But what if one of your songs turns out to be a hit? What if they start playing it in elevators? Because your songs could even end up in elevators, and it's really shitty to have to listen to them in an elevator. I could never imagine

MUSIC • When I think about music, I often see it in colors. There's gotta be enough blue so that the red looks good, and that decides how much yellow you use. Those are different colors, and I love those colors. When I was younger and took mushrooms, I could see music; the notes swirled around my body until I saw I was entangled in some kind of spiderweb, scattered with colorful notes, and I had become trapped. But, hey, music can never really be a trap. If you're an athlete—and this is the truth, I'm sorry to say—when you reach a certain age, your body gives up. But us musicians just get better till the end. And that's fantastic.

— SHERIFF —

listening to "Taxi Driver" in an elevator. It's still often standard procedure, so be warned never to mix your publishing deal and your record deal.

Then there are the percentages. The label always tells you you're a newcomer and they're taking a big risk by signing you, but the risk is not any bigger than with their older bands. When they're offering you the standard 12 to 16 percent, just ask for a 22 percent minimum or refuse to sign. If you're good enough, you will get your deal. They're pretending they're doing you a favor, but fuck them. If the band doesn't make money, it's a tax deduction for them.

It makes even more sense to record the album with your own money if you got the cash. It's advisable to first establish a corporation to produce the album. It does take about $55,000 minimum, though, and the band should be well-rehearsed and the songs should have been stripped down four, five times and reassembled again and again, until the best version has been found. Sometimes it might be the first version, sometimes the song just keeps getting better and better. But all it takes is a lot of hard work, and that's

KIRSI KOSKINEN

Yours for a while, live for a fee.

Andy McCoy 2001.

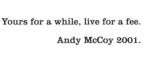

what being a musician is all about. This is hard work. People just see the glamorous side: big stages, fireworks, and helicopters. And those rare guitars you can never afford and wish you'd be able to just touch once in your life. This business is a shortcut to many things, because you can also make big money.

I have a friend whose first album sold thirteen million copies. Actually I have a couple friends in that band. One of them, the vocalist, is the so-called front man of the group, according to the press. I guess he's become the front man, since he's the only one left in the band. That's an example of what can happen when you get so much money so soon. In Hanoi, we slowly inched our way upwards. We were the last generation in Finland to tour the woodland dance pavilions, and the last generation in the world to tour before MTV really took full control of the market. Well, not full control, but they have a pretty good monopoly.

But you get nothing for free. This guy I'm talking about just went nuts because of the money. There had to be a limo and a bodyguard everywhere. Every once in a while he went to court for beating somebody up. It was pitiful. We messed up our finances in Hanoi when we were young, but at least we've grown wiser in that respect. At least Mike and me. When I talk with Mike these days, we're on the same wavelength. We've been doing this for so long. If the money makes you funny in the head, or if you're only in it for the cash, you should change the business. There are easier ways to make those millions, far easier ways. And there will be times when you won't have those millions in your bank account. Sometimes you might have nine months in

Right to left: Me, my wife, my mom, and my stepfather, Teukka,
who's the closest thing to a father figure I've ever had. My own dad
was a dunderhead Gypsy calo and naasko. Hello Soulfather, goodbye
biological moments of passion! My mother's happy.

between contracts when you're negotiating with a label, and you just have to borrow the money wherever you can. You become a full-time bum in order to make it to the next paycheck. And it gets infinitely worse if you've developed a drug problem. That's when the money really starts burning. You're not in control of anything, really. It's like you were drunk all the time—as I said, alcohol is a drug like any other. You really don't make the best deals if you're high as a kite when you're negotiating with these sober, hard-core business types. You're gonna end up with a deal that will most likely leave you sitting on a single chair in the kitchen of a single-room apartment, a warm beer and a cold sausage on the table, and an eviction notice on the door saying: "Move out within three days, asshole!"

Andy and a rickshaw. TUK...TUK...TUK...

Life can be tough, but I have no worries. As Dave Lindholm wrote in a song about me: "Andy takes care of the corner, he takes cares of his friends, too." Dave is a dear friend of mine. He has given me direction in my life when I've had no direction whatsoever. He has given me strength when I had no strength, and we've also had some fuckin' great times. Dave pretty much digs the same stuff I do. I don't think there are many old-timers around any more who know as much about old blues as he does. All these books I read in my youth weren't available back in the day. But hey, Dave's a well-read kid, too. Or maybe not a kid, but there's a little kid inside of Dave, too. And his brother's great. I can never forget Dave's brother, but Dave's the main man. Each time I've been down and out, Dave has told me: "Andy, you're so much better than these fuckin' garage rockers. You gotta go show 'em that this tradition continues, this attitude and this style."

I believe that rock 'n' roll is important not just for the fans. Even though it's culturally so underrated, it's still precious. More precious than an opera that's been performed everywhere for the last 300 years. You don't listen to that opera on the radio. Go ask people what's playing on their headphones, maybe one in ten thousand says he's listening to opera.

Even my good friend Lenny Kravitz wrote a song that claimed "Rock 'n' Roll Is Dead." But then why did he make it into a rock song? Lenny sold himself out on that song. Lenny, I'm sorry, but I think that was a bad mistake. Rock 'n' roll won't die as long as teenagers fall in love. Rock 'n' roll won't die as long as people want excitement in their lives. Rock 'n' roll won't die as long as kids want to rebel against their parents. Rock 'n' roll can mutate over the years, but still the most popular live bands play rock 'n' roll, from the Rolling Stones to AC/DC. I saw it again myself with Mike, when Hanoi Revisited played Ruisrock.

In Finland, rock 'n' roll has sort of reached puberty. Okay, we had Hurriganes and then Hanoi, both massive bands. You had Henry from Hurriganes and you had Andy. But Henry didn't have Mike, he had Cisse and Ape. But Ape started messin' around, and I guess Henry was under so much pressure that he didn't have the patience for somebody shitting all over a great band, all their great gigs. We always had Mike Monroe. He was our face. I didn't think I would get more recognition than the other guys—I just happened to be the songwriter, but at some point it just got way of hand. Suddenly I was a household name in Finland. Some things I did for fun, like this *Kokkisota* cooking show on TV that everybody seemed to like. I fucked up many interviews myself, and sometimes they wanted me to fuck up. Like this Rantalainen guy, who got me drunk before a live TV interview in front of the whole of Finland. I was about to pass out, and of course when Andy's nodding, everybody thinks it's because of heroin. As if I would've been in deep opium slumber—that was not the case at all.

GOD • Although so much was taken so early, I still believe in God. He's merciful and gave me so much hope, and he also gave me some direction.

The saddest thing in Finnish rock is that people just listen to certain kinds of songs. Even Eppu Normaali, who are supposed to be a rock band, just churn out these melancholy, minor-key, bullshit melodies. Couldn't they write a song that would make everybody feel good, a song that people could enjoy? Maybe they're just not able to write happy stuff. It's a thousand times more difficult to write that easy and happy song than those four-chord couplets Eppu Normaali keeps on rewriting.

What comes to other Finnish bands, I wish them all the luck. Especially HIM at the moment. Do it all the way, guys. And the 69 Eyes, you know where to find people who can help you write songs. You have a good label, after all. And of course Bomfunk MC's and Darude, all these Finnish artists that have recently had some visibility over here. But never forget: You wouldn't have the kind of record sales you have unless there had been guys like Remu Aaltonen from Hurriganes. And then, somewhere along the way, Dave Lindholm, followed by Andy McCoy and Mike Monroe and Hanoi Rocks.

I really don't know what tomorrow brings. I wish for something as great and explosive as Hanoi Rocks. It would prove to me that Finland is truly the future of rock 'n' roll. Without that, it's gonna be a phlegmatic place musically, where "same shit goes down, nothing changes around, it's a one-story town."

Lately I've been working on this book and reminiscing. Unfortunately, there were many stories I decided not to tell. Maybe their time will come in the future. I'm happy with my life. It's been rich and productive, and never so much as lately, when Mike and me started writing together again. I believe it's gonna work, just on the strength of the music. As long as we can both hold on to a certain character and vibe.

Some people are so sick and jealous that they destroy the energy of their own lives by drowning other people's vibes. But we're free as birds, Angela and me. The negativity is somewhere else, not in me, Michael, or Angela, but somewhere where it barely has the courage to show itself. And it won't show up here, because love, tolerance, and compassion live in my abode. Negativity is a guest that won't stay long before it's kicked out for good. In my home there's always room for friends. A lot of people have tried to abuse my hospitality, but I'm an old fuckin' fox by now; I can discern black from white. And the cards say that today's gonna be a great day.

165

— M c C o y —

DRUGS

People have just recently understood in Finland that drug addiction is totally comparable to alcoholism. But what are they doing about it? Alcoholics are not sent to prison but drug addicts still are. It's totally hypocritical. Okay, the people who are pushing dope could be jailed—especially the assholes who sell it to little kids. Apart from that, each adult should be able to decide for him- or herself what they're doing, as long as they don't hurt others.

Then there's stuff like hash. I think hash is simply an herb. There's nothing man-made about it; it's a clean, natural product. You should just use it like an herb, too. When Rastafaris smoke weed, it's to reach another dimension. They meditate. And it's also the only known medicine for asthma, anorexia nervosa, and other stuff. It's not much stronger than five cups of espresso. Then you have all this useless stuff like LSD that Mike and me eagerly sampled as kids. But would I do it again? No way. I've been there—I don't need to go back.

There have also been a shitload of designer drugs, Ecstasy, and whatnot, and I haven't tried them. Maybe I'm an old-time junkie, because I used just one, specific substance and had no interest whatsoever in other stuff.

When we talk about dope, or drugs in general, I've noticed one thing over the years, and it's that all substances you use to mess up your head are drugs. That means alcohol, too. Some of the them are human inventions, and those are usually the worst. Chemically refined poison. Take heroin, for example. It's made of raw opium. Opium is the raw material. First you create a morphine base, and you get morphine. Then you continue refining it until you have heroin. It's one of the best painkillers known to man, and I think it should only be used for medicinal purposes when you're in great pain. It's really not nice to wake up one morning and notice you've developed a heroin habit. It brings with itself horrible physical and mental pain.

Man has done the same thing to cocaine that he did to heroin. After all, people used coca leaves for thousands of years. Of course, white folks, as usual, separated this molecule that gives you the kick. It was refined and made into a real poison. Coke has some medical use, but I don't think it's for the people who don't need it, either.

Stimulants like amphetamine and methedrine that boost your blood circulation—your heart rate—so much that you don't eat or sleep—unless you're a longtime user whose tolerance is so high that you can lead a normal life and still use the stuff. But you can still see from their eyes and behavior if somebody's on speed. People stay up for five, six days, taking it until they collapse. Then they sleep for three, four days, and start all over again. Speed also brings out schizophrenia in a lot of people, and many have gone into amphetamine psychosis. I think amphetamine is one of the most horrible drugs ever invented, and methedrine is pretty much the same.

Then there's the psychedelic stuff like LSD, which I guess was already invented early in the last century, but rarely used until the hippie revolution. And when you drop acid, it gives you hallucinations. I've heard some people have stayed on that trip forever, though I've never met anybody like that. It means that they'd never be the same again. I also hear that some people get these flashbacks, but I've never met anyone like that either. It means that a trip you have already used would hit you again. I believe that's pretty much propaganda.

I used heroin for many, many years, and everything was okay as long as I had the merchandise. But oh man, when I ran out I became so sick, both physically and mentally, that nothing worked anymore. When I was using, I had papers to prove I was an incurable addict. That was false information too. I later met the doctor who used to supervise all the methadone clinics in Los Angeles county, and he said there's no such thing as an incurable addict.

I think that methadone is one of the worst drugs man has invented. It's an opiate that in its purest form is about fifty times more powerful than pure heroin. Withdrawal symptoms are also worse. It was originally meant to cure heroin addiction, but how can a substance that's fifty times stronger than heroin cure you from heroin addiction? That's something I don't understand. I've often noticed that people who use methadone eventually get hooked; and that monkey is so much more vicious than the heroin monkey on your back. Heroin addicts start getting better after being clean for a week, week and a half, but methadone addicts often have to be hospitalized. I've heard that in the worst cases, they have to stay hospitalized for almost a year. And that's it for the withdrawal symptoms.

It's extremely depressing to see how kids today use these designer drugs, Ecstasy and other shit. They're still so new that you don't even know what kind of damage they do, because you can only tell in ten years or so. Heroin—and this is something I understood a long time ago—is just merchandise. Some people make a fortune selling it. Once there's a market for a substance, you can be sure that there will always be people manufacturing the stuff. If somebody gets caught, there's someone else to take his place. That's one reason why I think this war on drugs can never be won. If there's demand, somebody will always take care of the supply, because there's so much money to be made.

When Mike and me were kids, I mean really young kids, we shared an overpowering urge to try everything. I guess so did everyone else in the band, more or less. I don't know how, but somehow it got divided so that Mike and me smoked weed, Nasse drank, and Sami and Razzle did both. Later on, some of us started doing speed and the others heroin. And neither one is better than the other.

Amphetamine and methedrine keep you awake and take away your hunger. As I told you, they can easily trigger a condition called schizophrenia. Paranoia is also very common among speed freaks. Heroin doesn't burn your brain in the same way, but it's so treacherous that one morning you just realize you've become totally addicted. It's really difficult. When you use it, you think like everyone else that you'll never get addicted, but one fine morning you wake up

and start wondering why you feel so shitty and can't even sleep. These are the early withdrawal symptoms. They just get worse the longer you use any kind of substance, so you will surely feel the fuckin' pain.

It was a relief to quit. I no longer have to be afraid when Mr. Cop comes and tells me to empty my pockets. I no longer have to worry where I'll get my fix for tomorrow. I no longer have to worry that I'll spend all my money on dope. When you're a heroin addict, your fix becomes a ritual. You remove the powder from the bag and sprinkle it on a spoon. If it's brown, you add some citric acid. If it's white, you just add water, hopefully sterilized water you can buy in a pharmacy in a 10ml ampule. The brown stuff you gotta heat up so that the citric acid will disintegrate the powder into pure liquid. When you heat up white heroin, it leaves no residue. It's white as water, whereas the brown heroin turns reddish brown. You stick the spike into your vein, inject it, and you'll basically feel orgasmic—if you can really say that, because it's much better. But I got so tired when I realized that it's just bullshit. It's so deceptive. Heroin's a nice distant cousin if you never meet, but it's a damn evil master. When it rules your life, you just leave everything for tomorrow. There's no hurry in the world, you just don't care, because you feel like a motherfuckin' king.

I've tried,
but never inhaled...2001.

OUTRO

I didn't tell all my stories in this book. Like how I worked with Alice Cooper when I was a twenty-two-year old kid, or how Mike and me went to Morocco for the first time. I obviously enjoyed being there for certain reasons. It was also great fun to play with Remu, although the Finnish evening papers have exaggerated and distorted our comments. Henry: *San mu phralo, tse calo hin tshinko! Fantastico!* Or about when we were at the Wailing Wall in Jerusalem and Hasidic Jews began to stone us. It was obviously because of Mike, because they thought Mike was a woman, and for some reason, men and women are supposed to be on the opposite sides of the wall. Anyway, about forty of these Hasidic Jews began to cry almost hysterically and throw stones at us. The army guys helped us with their machine guns. One of the soldiers told us that those people are pretty fanatic, so it's better to leave before the situation gets out of hand. As we ran away, I told Mike to show them his dick so they would calm down.

I also didn't tell you about the time when our bus broke down in the middle of nowhere in 100°F heat, or when we hired a mule to smuggle our dope so we wouldn't have to take the risk ourselves. Wow, life—I love it.

How many of you have said that I've been deep in shit up to my elbows? Well, it's true. Angela and me went to check out the Patpong district in Bangkok, the whore and nightlife center of the city. As we walked, I suggested to Angie that we take a shortcut through an alley. She was walking in front of me. It was completely dark, and all of a sudden the ground disappeared under my feet. What the fuck? I looked around and realized I was up to my neck in shit. I was in a sewer. Yikes!

THANKS • In this book I finally want to thank all those people who love music. Never start playing just because you want to get chicks or something. Play because you love music. If you do that, you have the chance to fuckin' share that love and spread good vibes around you, all these things I've tried to do. When this book comes out, I'll probably see some friends and a lot of sycophants at the book publishing party in Helsinki, but by now it has all become as familiar to me as flying on a Concorde, or a helicopter, or a 757. It's all transient—the only thing that remains is what you leave behind. Like this book. I hope this wasn't just a collection of crazy stories.

It was a nice neighborhood to go shit-diving, too: I watched as used condoms, needles, and other shit flowed past me. Of course I had on my brand-new silk suit, and diamond rings on my fingers. When I managed to climb up, I was completely covered with brown-green slime that stuck like a film. I found a water pipe and tried to wash the biggest turds away, but nothing seemed to help. It was nice to walk back to the hotel, because everybody steered right clear of me. Angela just laughed, but I was almost in tears. In the hotel room the brand-new, three-piece, silver-gray silk suit flew into a plastic bag and out of the door into the corridor.

I've been to heroin labs. I've been to bordellos, but I've never paid for a woman. I've been behind bars. I've been to the dark alleys of Kallio. I've been to the *barrio* in East L.A. I've been to Trenchtown in Kingston. Maybe the underworld and the slums attract me—at least, they did. I don't search for danger so eagerly anymore. I don't need it. I just want to write good songs and give people nice memories, good vibes, all beautiful things that may come. There's no way I want to be negative, although some lyrics are meant to be offensive to certain people. More than anything, they're supposed to be wake-up calls. Like, "Wake up! Don't you fucking realize what you're doing?" There are so many things wrong in this world, and you can't make them right, no matter how hard you try. But at least you can bring some joy in the world with music. That's something I've realized.

But there's still something I haven't told, something that can help you all. It's a Cherokee prayer I learnt from Angela's mother, and it goes something like this:

CHEROKEE PRAYER

Deep in the center of my being
There's an infinite well of love
I now allow this love to flow to the surface
It fills my heart, my soul, my body, my mind, my consciousness, my very being
And radiates out from me in all directions
And returns to me multiplied
The more love I use and give, the more love I have to give
The supply is endless
The use of love makes me feel good
It's an expression of my inner joy
I love myself
And therefore I take loving care of my body
I lovingly feed it with nourishing food and beverages
I lovingly groom and dress it
And my body lovingly responds to me with vibrant health and energy
I love myself
Therefore I provide myself a comfortable home
One that fills all my needs and is a pleasure to be in
I fill the rooms with the vibration of love
So that all who enter, myself included,
Will feel this love and be nourished by it
I love myself

Therefore I work at a job that I truly enjoy doing
One that uses my creative talents and abilities
Working with and for people who I love and who love me
And earning a good income
I love myself
Therefore I behave and think in a loving way to all people
For I know that that which I give out returns to me multiplied
I only attract loving people in my world
For they are a mirror of myself
I love myself
Therefore I forgive and totally release the past and all past experiences
And I am free
I love myself
Therefore I love totally in the now
Experiencing each moment as good
And knowing that my future is bright, joyous, and secure
For I am a beloved child of the universe
And the universe lovingly takes care of me
Now and forever more.
So let it be.

LOVE, ANDY

FOR KATALLE AND JUDY

They've now found Nirvana

Bathing in the fountain of love

My own recollections?

Full of beauty

When God asked you to come to him

An emptiness remained in my heart

That could never be filled

The streets are naked

Without your smile

And that laughter can no longer be heard

It's following the wind

In eternity

R.I.P.

ANDY

Kata Hulkko-Huhananti.

My sister, my brother's wife.

Mar. 11, 1964–Aug. 29, 2001

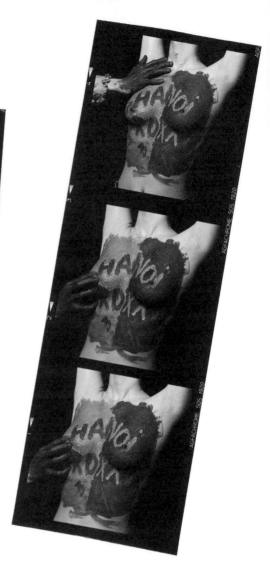

I give the breasts my fingers.
ORIENTAL BEAT back sleeve
photo session, sometime in '82.

ANDY McCOY
SELECT DISCOGRAPHY

The discography contains official releases in order of apperrance by grouping. Most promotional, non-commercial releases, and foreign pressings are not listed.

BRIARD

7" Singles:
I Really Hate You / I Want Ya Back (Delta DES 33) 1977
Fuck the Army / Product of TV Generation (Poko Rekords PIS 009) 1978
Chirpy Chirpy Cheep Cheep / Superstars (Love Records LRS 2241) 1979
Rockin' on the Beach / Miss World (Love Records LRS 2266) 1979
Fuck the Army (BMG 417772) 1996

Albums:
MISS WORLD *(Johanna JHN 3028) 1983*
    Backstreet Boys / Briard Song / James Dean Pop / TV Generation / Don't
    Turn the Pages / Fuck the Army / Me and My Habit / I Want Ya Back /
    The Life of Nasty / Miss World / Superstars / Finn Disc

ANDY McCOY & PETE MALMI: BRIARD
(BMG 74321417602) 1996
    Fuck the Army / I Didn't Know She Could Rock'n'Roll / River of Dreams
    / Let's Play Home / Why Is Love So Cruel / Sexy Girl / London Town /
    Head Over Heels / Border to Border / Spirit / Scream

MISS WORLD *(Johanna JHNCD 3028) 2005*
    Reissue of above with fifteen bonus songs.

PELLE MILJOONA OY

7" Singles:
Olen kaunis / Älä äiti itke (Johanna JHNS 125) 1980
Moottoritie on kuuma / Viesti (Johanna JHX 005, jukebox single) 1980

Albums:
MOOTTORITIE ON KUUMA *(Johanna JHNCD 2021) 1980*
Moottoritie on kuuma / Vapaus on suuri vankila / Meille kävi näin / Koska sydän sanoi niin / Kovat kundit / Olen kaunis / Juokse villi lapsi / Nuoret rakastavaiset / Älä äiti itke / Tänä yönä vien sut pois / Elämän pyörä / Moottoritie / Hyvää yötä maailma

PETE MALMI

7" Singles:
Suicide Sue / Rock 'n' Roll (Johanna JHNS 144) 1980
We Can Really Move Fast / Flight #1 (Johanna JHNS 186) 1980

Albums:
MALMI *(Johanna JHN 2048) 1980*

HANOI ROCKS

7", 12" & CD Singles:

I Want You / Kill City Kills (Johanna JHNS 145) 1980

Tragedy / Café Avenue (Johanna JHNS 174) 1981

Desperados / Devil Woman (Johanna JHNS 199) 1981

Dead by X-mas / Nothing New (Johanna JHNS 216) 1981

Love's an Injection / Taxi Driver (Johanna JHNS 244) 1982

Love's an Injection / Malibu Nightmare / Taxi Driver / Problem Child / In the Year '79 (Johanna JHEX 244 12") 1982

Until I Get You / Rebel on The Run (Johanna JHNS 534) 1983

Until I Get You / Rebel on The Run / Sailing Down The Tears (Johanna JHEX 534 12") 1983

Up Around the Bend / Until I Get You (AAB HANOIS 1) 1984

Up Around the Bend / Back to Mystery City / Until I Get You / Mental Beat (AAB HANOI X 1 12") 1984

Underwater World / Shakes / Magic Carpet Ride (AAB HANOI X2 12") 1984

People Like Me / Lucky / Winged Bull (Akashic Rocks ARCDS-001) 2002

A Day Late, A Dollar Short / Bad News / Moonlite Dance" (Major Leidén Productions MLCDS 003) 2003

Keep Our Fire Burning / Heaven Is Gonna Be Empty (Major Leidén Productions MLCDS 009) 2004

Back In Yer Face / Better High (Major Leidén Productions MLCDS 012) 2005

Fashion / Trouble Boys / Video: Fashion / Video: Boulevard of Broken Dreams (live) (WolfGang Records WOGCDS-001) 2007

Teenage Revolution / Self Destruction Blues (Backstage Alliance BSACD010) 2008

Albums:

BANGKOK SHOCKS SAIGON SHAKES HANOI ROCKS
(Johanna JHNCD 2037) 1981
*Tragedy / Village Girl / Stop Cryin' / Don't Never Leave Me / Lost in the
City / First Timer / Cheyenne / 11th Street Kids / Walking with My Angel
/ Pretender; CD Bonus: I Want You / Kill City Kills / Café Avenue /
Desperados / Dead by X-mas / Nothing New*

ORIENTAL BEAT (Johanna JHNCD 2063) 1982
*Motorvatin' / Don't Follow Me / Visitor / Teenangels Outsiders / Sweet Home
Suburbia / MC Baby / No Law or Order / Oriental Beat / Devil Woman
/ Lightnin' Bar Blues / Fallen Star; CD Bonus: Love's an Injection / Malibu
Nightmare / Taxi Driver / Problem Child / In the Year 1979*

SELF DESTRUCTION BLUES (Johanna JHN 3008) 1982
*Love's an Injection / I Want You / Café Avenue / Nothing New / Kill City
Kills / Self Destruction Blues / Beer and a Cigarette / Whispers in the Dark /
Taxi Driver / Desperados / Problem Child / Dead by X-mas*

BACK TO MYSTERY CITY (Johanna JHNCD 3023) 1983
*Strange Boys Play Weird Openings / Malibu Beach Nightmare / Mental Beat
/ Tooting Bec Wrecked / Until I Get You / Sailing Down the Tears / Lick
Summer Love / Beating Gets Faster / Ice Cream Summer / Back to Mystery
City*

ALL THOSE WASTED YEARS (Johanna HANOICD 1) 1984
*Pipeline / Oriental Beat / Back to Mystery City / Motorvatin' / Until I Get
You / Mental Beat / Don't You Ever Leave Me / Tragedy / Malibu Beach
Nightmare / Visitor / 11th Street Kids / Taxi Driver / Lost in the City /
Lightnin' Bar Blues / Beer and a Cigarette / Under My Wheels / I Feel Alright
/ Train Kept a Rollin'*

Two Steps From the Move *(AAB HANOICD 2) 1984*
*Up Around the Bend / High School / I Can't Get It / Underwater World /
Don't You Ever Leave Me / Million Miles Away / Boulevard of Broken Dreams
/ Boiler (Me Boiler 'n' Me) / Futurama / Cutting Corners*

Rock 'n' Roll Divorce *(Lick BOOTLIC 7) 1985*
*Two Steps from the Move / Back to Mystery City / Boulevard of Broken
Dreams / Don't You Ever Leave Me / Tragedy / Malibu Beach Nightmare /
Million Miles Away / Taxi Driver / Up Around the Bend / I Feel Alright /
Rock & Roll / Looking at You*

Twelve Shots on the Rocks
(Major Leidén Productions MLCD-001) 2002
*Intro / Obscured / Whatcha Want / People Like Me / In My Darkest
Moment / Delirious / A Day Late, A Dollar Short / New York City / Winged
Bull / Watch This / Gypsy Boots / Lucky / Designs on You / Up in Smoke*

Another Hostile Takeover
(Major Leidén Productions MLCD 013) 2005
*Intro / Back in Yer Face / Hurt / The Devil in You / Love / Talk to the Hand
/ Eternal Optimist / No Compromise, No Regrets / Reggae Rocker / You Make
the Earth Move / Better High / Dear Miss Lonely Hearts / Center of My
Universe*

Street Poetry *(WolfGang Records WOGCD005) 2007*
*Hypermobile / Street Poetry / Fashion / Highwired / Power of Persuasion /
Teenage Revolution / Worth Your Weight in Gold / Transcendental Groove /
This One's for Rock 'N' Roll / Powertrip / Walkin' Away / Tootin' Star /
Fumblefoot and Busy Bee*

Compilations

THE BEST OF HANOI ROCKS *(YAHOO HANOI LP 3) 1985*
 (Original release contains bonus four-song 12" EP)

MILLION MILES AWAY *(Mercury/Nippon Phonogram) 1986*

DEAD BY CHRISTMAS *(Raw Power RAWLP 016 double LP) 1986*

THE COLLECTION *(AAB-Tuotanto AABCD4) 1989*

UP AROUND THE BEND *(Mercury/Nippon Phonogram CD) 1989*

HANOI ROCKS STORY *(Mercury/Nippon Phonogram CD) 1990*
 (features interview snippets between songs)

TRACKS FROM A BROKEN DREAM *(Lick Records LICLP 10) 1990*

STRANGE BOYS PLAY WEIRD OPENINGS
 (Mercury/Nippon Phonogram 4-CD set) 1991

LEAN ON ME *(Lick Records LIC CD 11) 1992*

ALL THOSE GLAMOROUS YEARS *(Mercury/PolyGram Japan) 1996*

DECADENT DANGEROUS DELICIOUS *(Essential!/Castle UK) 2000*

KILL CITY KILLS *(Delta UK 47 041) 2000*

HANOI ROCKS 4-CD BOX SET *(Johanna 2524) 2001*

UP AROUND THE BEND, THE DEFINITIVE COLLECTION
 (Sanctuary Records UK SMEDD 002 double CD) 2004

LIGHTNIN' BAR BLUES, THE ALBUMS 1981-1984
 (Castle Music UK CMXBX1104) 2005 (6-CD box set)

THIS ONE'S FOR ROCK'N'ROLL/THE BEST OF HANOI ROCKS
 (Johanna Kustannus/Backstage Alliance BSACD-020 2-CD) 2008

CHERRY BOMBZ

12" Singles:

"Hot Girls in Love" / "100 Degrees in the Shade" / "Feline Feeling" / "Oil &
    Gasoline" / "Pin-Up Boy" (YAHOOLP 101) 1985
"House Of Ecstasy" / "Countryfied Inner City Blues" / "Running (Back to Your
    Lover)" (YAHOOX 2) 1986

Albums:

COMING DOWN SLOW (LIVE) *(High Dragon HD021) 1987*
    *Intro / House of Ecstasy / 100 Degrees in the Shade / Pin-Up Boy /
    Life's Been Hard / Oil & Gasoline / Sweet Pretending / Coming Down
    Slow / Gimme Good Loving / Hot Girls in Love / Ain't What You Do /
    Travellin' Band CD-bonus: Lips of Love / Taxi Driver*

THE SUICIDE TWINS

Albums:

SILVER MISSILES AND NIGHTINGALES
    (YAHOOCD 102) 1986
    *Dance / Heaven Made You / Declaration / Mainline Service / What a Price
    to Pay / Silver Missiles and Nightingales / Coming Down Slow / The Best
    Is Yet to Come / Sweet Pretending / Countryfied Inner City Blues*

ANDY McCOY

7" Singles:
"I Will Follow" / "Make Believe" (Amulet HOPE 46) 1988
"Too Much Ain't Enough" / "Knee Deep in Sky High"
    (Amulet HOPE 66) 1991
"Strung Out" / "I'm Gonna Roll You" / "Unconditional Love"
    (AMTXCD 214) 1995
"Let It Rock" / "Heart Attack" / "Candle Burnt Down"
    (AMTXCD 218) 1995

Albums:
TOO MUCH AIN'T ENOUGH (Amulet WISHCD 6) 1988
    I Will Follow / Tell Me a Story / Talking 'Bout a Feeling / Knee Deep in
    Sky High / Too Far Gone / Too Much Ain't Enough / Spanish Harlem /
    My Mistake / Heart of The Matter / Make Believe

BUILDING ON TRADITION (AMTCD 2069) 1995
    Strung Out / I'm Gonna Roll You / Born Again Electric / She's Doing It
    With Lazers / Unconditional Love / Foxfield Junction / Heart Attack /
    Love & Hate / Dreaming of Japan / Let It Rock / Italian Girl / Gotta
    Let It Go / Apache / Medieval Madras

THE REAL McCOY OST (Megamania 1000 121072) 1999
    Mind Over Matter / Through the Eyes of a Child / Tragedy (Hanoi Rocks)
    / Keys to Heaven / Shadow Chasing / Strung Out / Inner City Bleeds
    / Super McFly / Don't You Ever Leave Me (Hanoi Rocks) / The Real
    McCoy / Annan kitaran laulaa vaan / River Of Dreams / Shiva

Compilations:

ASPECTS OF ANDY McCOY *(Polarvox WISHCD 50) 1995*
Hot Girls in Love (Cherry Bombz) / Backstreet Boys (Briard) / Sweet Pretending (Suicide Twins) / I Will Follow (Andy McCoy) / Briard Song (Briard) / Brown Eyed Girl (Shooting Gallery) / Running (Back to Your Love) (Cherry Bombz) / Miss World (Briard) / Little Bit of Magic (Shooting Gallery) / Restless (Shooting Gallery) / Fuck the Army (Briard) / House of Ecstasy (Cherry Bombz) / What a Price to Pay (Suicide Twins) / Nature of My Business (Shooting Gallery) / My Mistake (Andy McCoy) / Me and My Habit (Briard) / Dandelion (Shooting Gallery) / The Best Is Yet to Come (Suicide Twins) [First pressing contains bonus disc: THE BEST OF HANOI ROCKS]

R'N'R MEMORABILIA, THE BEST SOLO TRACKS SO FAR *(Capitol/EMI International 7243 5915912 6) 2003*
Strung Out / I Didn't Know She Could Rock 'N' Roll (feat. Pete Malmi) / Oil & Gasoline (Cherry Bombz) / Silver Missiles & Nightingales (Suicide Twins) / Mind Over Matter / Nature of My Business (Shooting Gallery) / Fuck the Army (feat. Pete Malmi) / Product of TV Generation (Briard) / River of Dreams (feat. Pete Malmi) / Love & Hate / What a Price To Pay (Suicide Twins) / Through the Eyes of a Child / Real McCoy / Dandelion (Shooting Gallery) / Born Again Electric / I Really Hate Ya (Briard) / My Mistake / Hot Girls in Love (Cherry Bombz) / Border to Border (feat. Pete Malmi) / Best Is Yet to Come (Suicide Twins) / Sweet Pretending (Suicide Twins) / I Mess Around (Shooting Gallery) / Striptease (Shooting Gallery) / She's Doing It With Lazers / Apache / Inner City Bleeds / Medieval Madras / Head Over Heels (feat. Pete Malmi) / Restless (Shooting Gallery) / Leave Me Alone (Shooting Gallery) / I Will Follow / Too Much Ain't Enough / Anna Kitaran Laulaa (feat. Dave Lindholm)

SHOOTING GALLERY

Albums:

SHOOTING GALLERY *(Amulet WISHCD 45) 1992*
   *Restless / Teenage Breakdown / Nature of My Business / Don't Never Leave
   Me / Little Bit of Magic / I Mess Around / Striptease / Brown Eyed Girl
   / Devil Calling / Leave Me Alone / Dandelion*

WITH IGGY POP

In 1988–1989 Andy toured with Iggy Pop as guitarist on the Instinct tour, and
his playing can be heard on the following live releases:

IGGY POP: LIVE AT THE CHANNEL, BOSTON MA 1988 (NEW ROSE BLUES 4041) 1995
   *Instinct / Kill City / 1969 / Penetration / Power and Freedom / Your Pretty Face /
   High on You / Five Foot One / Johanna / Easy Rider / Tuff Baby / 1970 / Search and
   Destroy / Squarehead / No Fun / I Wanna Be Your Dog*

IGGY POP: BEST OF... LIVE (MCA/BMG MCD 84021/BM 640) 1996
   *Raw Power * / High on You * / Nightclubbin' / China Girl / Blah Blah Blah / No Fun
   / 1969 */ TV Eye / Easy Rider * / I Need Somebody / Five Foot One * / I Wanna Be
   Your Dog * / The Passenger * / I Got a Right * / Some Weird Sin / Real Wild Child /
   Lust for Life / Search and Destroy * [* Tracks featuring Andy]*

IGGY POP: KING BISCUIT—FLOWER HOUR PRESENTS IGGY POP
   (KBFH Records/BMG 70710-88033-2) 1997
   *Instinct / Kill City / 1969 / Penetration / Power and Freedom / High on You / Five
   Foot One / Johanna / Easy Rider / Tuff Baby / I Feel Alright (1970) / Winners and
   Losers / Scene of the Crime/ Search and Destroy / Cold Metal / Squarehead / No Fun /
   I Wanna Be Your Dog*

Guest Appearances

In addition to his bands and solo projects, Andy McCoy has recorded numerous guest appearances, including:

Maukka Perusjätkä: Ennen kolmatta maailmansotaa
   (Johanna JHN 2025) 1980 (guitar/songwriting)

Urban Dogs: Urban Dogs (Fallout FALL 012) 1983
   A Bridge Too Far / Human Being (guitar)

Yasuaki Honda: Angel of Glass (Philips LP) 1983
   Keep Our Fire Burning (guitar)

Fallen Angels (Fallout FALL 0022) 1984
   (additional guitar)

UK Subs: Killing Time (Fallout) 1989
   Drag Me Down (additional guitar)

Snatches of Pink: Bent With Pray (Caroline) 1992
   Screams (acoustic guitar)

69 Eyes: Savage Garden (Cleopatra) 1995
   Wild Talk (guitar/songwriting)

69 Eyes: Velvet Touch EP (Ga Ga Goodies / Poco Records) 1995
   TV Eye (guitar)

XL5: Taas mennään
   Nyt mennään (GT version featuring Andy McCoy) (guitar)

Stranded in the Doll's House: Tribute to J. Thunders & J. Nolan
   (Hurtin Recs) 1997 *Vietnamese Baby* (w/69 Eyes)

Discography compiled by Anssi Mehtälä. Thanks to Jukka Halonen, Jukka Nissinen, Joseph Schafer, and Johnny Burner.

VIKASIVU
JA FINITO

Love
xxx